THE
SCHOOLYARD
BULLY

Kim Zarzour

THE
SCHOOLYARD
BULLY

HarperCollins*Publishers*Ltd

Canadian Cataloguing in Publication Data

Zarzour, Kim
The schoolyard bully:
how to cope with conflict and raise an
assertive child

ISBN 0-00-638519-2

1. Assertiveness in children. 2. Bullying.
3. Child rearing. I. Title.

BF637.B85Z37 1999   649'.7   C99-932218-4

99 00 01 02 03 04 RRD 6 5 4 3 2 1

Printed and bound in the United States

To my husband

Wind in my sails,
port in a storm.

*The strong man is the man who can stand up
for his rights and not hit back.*

– Dr. Martin Luther King, Jr.

CONTENTS

Preface

For the longest time I kept it hidden, vaguely ashamed, assuming somehow it was my own fault. Only now, with kids of my own, do I feel comfortable coming out of the closet. I was a schoolyard victim. A bully-ee. The one the tough kids loved to pick on.

Every morning, before the first bell rang to usher us into our junior-high classrooms, I'd huddle against the brick wall outside and wait. Soon enough, they'd saunter over: big Jane, mean Carol and tag-along Sue. They always wore black, dyed their bangs blonde and lived to humiliate.

"Whatcha got for us today, Kimmeee?" They'd grab my yellow lunch pail. (I eventually learned to hand it to them as soon as I saw them coming.) Out came the boring stuff—the tuna sandwich, the apple, the banana. Then they'd whoop with delight and my heart would sink. They had discovered the brownies, the cookies, some special treat my mother had baked for me and, if I was really unlucky, a little encouraging note Mom had slipped in to give me a mid-day boost.

Off they'd go with their treasures, showing the laughing world my mom's note, leaving me to pick up my lunch-box leftovers.

I never cried. I never fought back. I never told my mom.

I guess I was chosen because I was skinny, shy, a "goody two shoes." I always figured my best defence was to be really nice. If I was nice enough, I reasoned, maybe they'd leave me alone.

Not a chance. As the school year progressed, so did the bullying, until one morning I found myself being sat on while the boys kicked snow in my face. That finally broke me. I cried. One of the girls quietly apologized and begged me not to tattle. When the teacher demanded to know why I was late, I made some other excuse, defended my tormentors and took the rap on my own.

After that they left me alone—with a bruised ego that would take several years to heal.

My childhood trauma wasn't unique. In fact child development experts say as many as half of all children experience pain at the hands of a schoolyard bully. And they are worried because the attacks are becoming more serious—and leaving lasting emotional scars.

My schoolyard persecution is long past now and I've come through relatively unscathed, but there are countless victims out there still nursing their wounds, countless children still cringing under the bully's power. I have written this book for them. Childhood needn't be so cruel.

Acknowledgments

A bully doesn't become a bully on his own. Neither does a book become a book by itself. There are so many people who helped me so greatly on this book, I couldn't begin to list all their names here. But to name just a few.

First and foremost, I want to thank fellow author and parent extraordinaire Sharon McKay, whose inspiration, encouragement and sense of humor nosed me along. Thanks also to my editor and publisher, Iris Skeoch, for being gentle with a rookie and my editor Susan Broadhurst for her clarity of thought.

Thanks to my readers who offered their time and considerable knowledge: Dr. Fred Mathews, Community Psychologist/Director of Research, Central Toronto Youth Services and an associate with the Department of Applied Psychology, Ontario Institute for Studies in Education/University of Toronto; Dr. Debra Pepler, a psychology professor at York University; Dr. Peter Sutton, head of the Infant Psychiatry Program at Toronto's Hospital for Sick Children; and Sandra Campbell, educational researcher with VIVA Associates.

I also wish to extend special thanks to the following experts for their input and expertise: Dr. Richard E. Tremblay, Director of the Research Unit on Children's Psychosocial Maladjustment, Faculté des Arts et des Sciences, Universite de Montréal; Dr. Arlette Lefebvre, psychiatrist at Toronto's Hospital for Sick Children; Dr. Dan Olweus, professor in the Division of Personality and Developmental Psychology at the University of Bergen; Dr. David G. Perry, Professor of Psychology at Florida's Atlantic University; Dr. Alice Charach, with the C. M. Hincks Research Institute; Dr. Lisa A. Serbin, with the Centre for Research in Human Development and Department of Psychology at Concordia University; and Dr. David Farrington with the Institute of Criminology at the University of Cambridge. Also, there are numerous other educators, parents, psychologists and social scientists who took time to explain their research, ideas and observations to me. Thank you. And thanks to Parentbooks for helping me put together the Recommended Reading lists.

My deepest thanks, however, go to the victims and bullies who shared their intimate, honest, often heart-wrenching stories with me. For many it was extremely difficult to rehash those painful memories. It is my strongest hope that by speaking out about their experiences they will touch others and inspire change.

Finally, I would like to thank Stephanie Thorens, Alyssa Gourley, and Doug and Ingrid Davis for their availability and unwavering sanity. And of course, my family—my readers, my critics, my cheerleaders.

THE
SCHOOLYARD
BULLY

1

The Nature of Bullying

Until the horrible spring of 1999, schoolyard bullying was a bit of a non-issue. Kids bullied. Kids got bullied. Fact of life and no big deal. Except for a few more enlightened souls, educators and child psychologists, the world did what it has always done when little people torment other little people—it looked the other way.

Then the unthinkable happened.

Two teenage boys in Littleton, Colorado, deeply troubled by years of exclusion and teasing, suddenly exploded in a deadly attack on their classmates and themselves. By the time they finished their revenging rampage and had turned their weapons upon themselves, they had killed 15 and wounded many more. It was the worst school massacre in the country's history.

Then, as if to prove this was not unique to the United States, not a symbol of one country's overly aggressive culture, an onslaught of victim outrage fell like demonic dominos around the world. At a peaceful rural school in Alberta a bullied boy shot two students, killing one.

Before Littleton, similar school violence had already exploded in Kentucky, Arkansas, Mississippi, California, Oregon and Pennyslvania. Now the toxin spread to blue-collar towns, prairie farmlands and well-to-do suburbs, from a small town in Britain to Tokyo, Japan, to a proliferation of website hitlists, death threats, attempted bombings and warnings scrawled on washroom walls.

Suddenly those good old golden rule days lost their gilded innocence; childhood aggression wasn't such an ignorable issue any more. Those who had been laboring on the sidelines for years saw violence in the schools move front and centre with helpless urgency—and a cacophony of explanations. Everyone scrambled for scapegoats, Hollywood or guns or the Internet, climbing all over each other for answers, screaming about trench-coats and metal detectors, see-through backpacks and fortress-like schools. Prayers were re-invited into the classroom, parents re-encouraged to spank. And while many called for crackdowns on the "freaks," "sickos" and "losers," others struggled to understand a hidden world where if you don't fit in, you're eaten alive.

Will this be another flash-in-the-pan media event? Will bullying be buried again after everyone forgets? Only time will tell. But when something similar happened 17 years ago in Norway, the public was galvanized into action. Less than a year after three bullied boys committed suicide, the country launched a national campaign in all primary and junior schools that today stands as a model for success. Experts on schoolyard bullying hope something similar will happen here, that something good will come of something so tragic.

"I remember how they used to tease me about my red hair. They made me feel so very ugly!" Anne*, a mother of two, self-consciously puts her hand to her beautiful red coiffure. "I wonder sometimes if that affected how I feel about myself now, in subtle ways that I'm not aware of. I do know one thing—I'd do anything to keep my own kids from feeling the same kind of pain."

Most parents know instinctively that childhood social experiences are very important. They sense that those first relationships are lessons that will take their children through life. So when things go wrong—when a child isn't fitting in or, worse, is being excluded or abused at the hands of his or her peers—the experience can be excruciating.

And parents don't know the half of it. Much of childhood bullying goes unreported and unrectified, buried beneath a complicated code of silence that muffles little "tattletales." Children who witness and are troubled by violence against other children don't know how, or even if, they should help. To them the adult world is uncaring and ineffective, too busy rushing about at a distance to understand what's really going on.

This book looks at just that: what's really going on at recess, on the bus, in the halls and in the malls. It looks at the typical bully and victim, and examines the sort of adults they grow up to be. And it offers suggestions for parents to raise assertive—not aggressive—children, youngsters who are strong enough to avoid being a bully or being bullied. The examples you'll read about run the gamut from the garden-variety name-calling classmate to the teenage gang, that armed, amorphous, anonymous big

*Names have been changed throughout to protect the privacy of the individuals in these personal accounts.

bully of the 1990s. And it will point out how the two extremes may be dangerously linked.

CHANGING ATTITUDES TOWARDS BULLYING

The bully wasn't always someone of ill repute. In the 16th century the word "bully" meant sweetheart. Gradually the bully's rank slipped. "Bully" came to mean a "fine fellow," then "blusterer" and finally today's "harasser of inferiors." Grandma or Grandpa probably ran into bullies. Their grandparents probably have their own bully stories, and their grandparents before them. In fact the story of evolution and Darwin's survival of the fittest is, in a sense, a story of bullies—the age-old struggle to be top of the heap, whatever the cost.

Like it or not, the bully's place in this world is firmly entrenched. The ritual childhood humiliation continues in playgrounds and school yards everywhere. So does the debate among parents. On one side of the fence are the moms and dads whose protective instincts click in when their child is under attack. They see red. On the other side are the parents who shrug it off as an unavoidable part of growing up. Not fun, but hey, it happens to everyone, as much a part of childhood as skinned knees and pimply faces.

New research puts that idea to shame. The bully is doing long-term damage, to himself, to his victims, to his fellow classmates. Bullying is not something children grow out of.

- The damage is devastating and long-lasting.
- Both victims and bullies need help.
- One in three schoolchildren may be involved in bullying at any one time.

• Children who witness bullying are getting dangerous
lessons in the acceptance of violence.

Much of the research on bullying is so new that the average educator isn't aware of it and therefore doesn't know
about its implications. It's only been in the last 30 years
or so that the bully phenomenon has been studied
systematically, first in Scandinavia, then in Britain and
Japan, now in North America and worldwide.

However, parents who remember their run-ins with the
school bully nostalgically just can't see what the fuss is all
about. For them it's a quick, convenient little lesson in life.

*"It was 1930 and I was ten years old," Cecil
remembers. "In the school yard was a husky kid
named Sidney who liked to pick on kids who were
smaller than him. One day, as I struggled with
him, I managed to grab his little finger and
twisted it with all my might. He went down
screaming. I never knew if his finger was
damaged, but it did end his days of being a bully.
Nobody else bothered me either. The experience
taught me the value of standing up for myself."*

But that was then.
This is now:
Staff at a nice junior high school in a comfortable
suburban neighborhood discover students have been
hiding rifles in a school ceiling as "protection" against
bullying gangs from other schools. In the countryside,
house parties are trashed by groups of teenage bullies. In
the city, students steal cell phones and designer jackets
off their schoolmates' backs for the "rush," the thrill, of

beating up another child. In Toronto, parents line up in the middle of the night, camping outside schools in sub-zero weather at registration time, putting unborn kids on waiting lists and forking out $1,000 apiece in transportation costs just to ensure their children can attend schools with a reputation for discipline and minimal violence. In Vancouver, students make sure they're surrounded by friends for protection. And in a rural school in a small town in northern Canada, a dispute over a bully's girlfriend snowballs into a pitched battle with a bored and bloodthirsty pubescent mob.

This tyrannizing of the timid is happening everywhere, sometimes with fatal results. The Colorado tragedy was not the first. In Canada, a teenage victim of bullying throws himself onto the subway tracks. In the U.S., a 15-year-old student, tired of being teased about being short, shoots and kills his tormentor in biology class. In Japan, where victims have been made to swallow weeds and milk laced with detergent, several students die or kill themselves each year from sadistic bullying by classmates and teachers. In Tokyo, three boys were sent to a reformatory for the death of a 13-year-old classmate who suffocated after being left wrapped upside down in an exercise mat. And in a Montreal suburb, four teenage victims of "taxing" (extortion by bullies) killed themselves, leaving behind this note: "My dream is to be free to go where I want to without any fear."

And yet the horror stories don't tell it all. There are subtle, almost invisible effects on those who have been bullied, members of the walking wounded whose external bruises may have faded but who continue to carry internal evidence of their pain. There are psychological bruises: a lack of self-confidence, depression and shame.

Even after the victims of bullying have grown up, it's hard for many of them to speak about their humiliation. They are still embarrassed, still feel as if it was their fault, and retelling the story can bring back waves of degradation. The bully's taunting laugh is never very far away.

THE LONG-TERM EFFECTS OF BULLYING

> *He was the Grade 6 bully and everyone knew it. That was many years ago. He and his classmates have grown up now and have lives of their own. His is in a federal penitentiary. A few years ago he stabbed a little girl to death. His schoolmates weren't surprised. They saw the warning signs in the playground 30 years ago.*

The prognosis is not good. The schoolyard bully is on a crash course with the future. Research shows the bully will continue to plow through life leaving damage in his wake. And many, like this Grade 6 bully, will end up with a criminal record. The prognosis is pretty dismal for the victim too. His childhood pain may dog him through his life and gnaw at his relationships as an adult.

Studies carried out around the world point to alarming trends. Among bullies:

- About 60 per cent of boys who were characterized as bullies in Grades 6 through 9 ended up with at least one criminal conviction by the age of 24. Bullies are four times more likely than non-bullies to be involved in serious repetitive criminal activities.— University of Bergen, Norway.
- Males who were bullies in adolescence tended to be

bullies in adulthood. By age 18, they continued to be highly delinquent and antisocial, and as adults they were likely to be heavy gamblers and smokers. They also were likely to have children who were bullies.— Cambridge University.

- At age 19, those who were most aggressive as eight-year-olds were more likely to have dropped out of school and have criminal records. At age 30, they were more likely to have children of their own who were aggressive.—University of Illinois, Chicago.

- Kids who bully in elementary school are more likely to perpetrate sexual harassment, commit date violence in their first relationship, join gangs and become juvenile delinquents. They are also likely to drop out of school, become teenage parents, have difficulty parenting, punish their children harshly and get involved in criminal activity. Dr. Wendy Craig, along with colleagues Dr. Jennifer Connolly and Dr. Debra Pepler from York University, is following 1,800 children from 10 to 14 years of age. Their preliminary results show that children involved in bullying are more likely to be involved in sexual harassing and physically aggressive behavior when they reach adolescence and begin dating. Surprisingly, both girls who are bullies and girls who are victims tend to date boys who are bullies.

The evidence is clear. Children who have problems with aggression when young have problems with aggression as adults. It makes sense; if they experience success as a bully in school, then there is a good chance they'll try it out elsewhere, in other spheres in their lives—with their colleagues at work, in spouse and child abuse. The schoolyard bully becomes an abusive adult caught in poor relationships and dead-end jobs. As the bully grows older, he often plunges from the top of the schoolyard totem pole to the bottom. What made him popular before makes him unpopular later. Often, when he reaches late adolescence, he loses his footing in the mainstream until the only ones who accept him are those with similar temperaments. Grouped together, the outcasts tend to reinforce their bad behavior, and unchecked, feed off each other's aggressiveness, becoming increasingly mean-spirited, violent, even suicidal. Some studies show bullies are more prone to depression and serious thoughts of suicide.

Victims also fare badly. In the short term, the victim feels not only the bully's actual bruises but psychological distress as well, facing every morning with a dismal hangover of fear. The distress can be psychosomatic: those vague aches and pains that make him want to stay in bed. Then school work suffers because he is too afraid to go to school, skips classes or persuades mom he's sick. In fact, the National Association of School Psychologists estimates 160,000 children miss school every day in the United States for fear of being bullied. What's more, even if he does venture back to class, he can't concentrate with the bully's eyes (real or imagined) boring holes through the back of his head.

But the victim carries other scars that last a lifetime. One man, who says his childhood years in a posh boarding school were a nightmare of cruelty, believes he will never get over it.

"I remember one day Ned decided to repeatedly slam my lower back against a radiator grill until I was semi-conscious. He also took great delight

in waiting until I was just about to exit the bus and then he would deliberately reach over the front seat and vomit onto my navy trench coat. The same boy pushed me into a pile of vomit on the locker-room floor. Another time a bully forced me to remain seated on a toilet with my pajamas still on and buttoned while a large amount of poop soiled them and me. I was trembling with fear and rage.

"All I went through at school has made me too frightened to trust what people say and to meet new people. I am very depressed and my self-esteem is battered, likely forever. At critical moments, I feel as though people judge me as a pushover. This no doubt has affected my career prospects as well as many daily activities. My peers at work have always said I wasn't tough enough, too kind, a pushover. I feel I can't change this perception so I am resigned to being what I am.

"I'm very tired most times. I'm lucky to be employed but I'm underemployed, so the days are a waste of my intelligence. I'm fortunate to have a lovely wife and a three-and-a-half-year-old daughter, but the past is still saddening and maddening. I used to say, 'I want to grow old very quickly' so that no one could contradict me or give me negative answers or arrogant advice. Life can be so cruel and insensitive. I'm despairing, sad."

Being a victim may be especially tough on boys, perhaps because it is so contrary to society's expectations of male strength. And these boys' children in turn stand a good chance of becoming victims too. According to a Cambridge

University study, boys who were lonely, nervous and unpopular in adolescence were more likely to have children who were also victims of bullying.[1]

But victims of both sexes who suffer childhood social isolation tend to continue to feel isolated in adulthood. The harassment may stop, now that they are more free to choose their own environment and companions. But the pain still echoes in their minds and colors the way they feel about themselves. In a follow-up study of 23-year-old men who had been schoolyard victims, some of them for at least three years, Norwegian psychologist Dr. Dan Olweus discovered low self-esteem and high levels of depression long after the bullying stopped. Seven to ten years later they were still feeling lousy about themselves. Olweus' tests show that victims were not born this way; rather, these characteristics are a direct result of the bullying they suffered when they were young.

But there are other actors in this playground drama. The children who watch the bully-victim interactions are learning too—learning that might is right, that it doesn't pay to interfere, that you'd better pick your friends for their strength and clout, not for their loyalty or shared interests.

And when bullying continues unabated, the victim unaided by grownups, children lose their faith in the adult world. They come to the conclusion that they are forsaken, they are on their own. It's not a big stretch to the jacket-swarming, curb-stomping, house-trashing and mass-murdering crimes of today's teenage world.

PARENTAL ATTITUDE TO BULLYING IS THE KEY

In this increasingly violent world, the most difficult obstacle standing in the way of schoolyard peace may be that grownups' own approach to the problem is often based on their own bullying experiences and only makes the problem worse.

The parents who subscribe to "the best defence is offence" are one example: a good right jab and the bully is history. One father remembers a confrontation with his boyhood bully with a feeling of pride: "Somehow, in my terror, I found the strength to draw back and land one good punch before taking flight," he recounts with relish. "The bully never bothered me again." The father made sure to pass on his triumph and wisdom to his son and grandson. "If you want to stop a bully," he advised them, "be sure to make that first blow count."

Child development experts disagree. In today's aggressive climate, in which violence begets more violence, that pat advice only reinforces the credo that Might is Right. And there are many children who just don't have it in them to fight back physically. A bout with the bully is not a simple rite of passage, a way of standing up for yourself. Assertiveness is an essential skill in today's world, but it is not acquired with fists. It is learned gradually, as a child grows up feeling good about himself and empathetic towards others. This book shows how grownups can instill that assertiveness in their children using compassion and commitment, and relegate the bully to a dark spot in the history books.

2

Understanding the Bully

"During my Grade 5 year, a wealthy family moved into the neighborhood," Roger remembers. "Their son, Evan, was a quiet, retiring chap, my age. I immediately sensed that he would not fight back.

"The bullying started gradually. During recess, most of the boys played British Bulldog. Initially Evan didn't want to play. He shied away from physical contact, even in phys. ed. when the teacher was at least monitoring events. I started the razzing. 'C'mon man, don't be a wimp. Everyone's playing. Even some girls!' He eventually played. Well, when I was 'it,' I went for Evan right away. He likely realized that I would target him and didn't put up much of a fight. When I got him, I really roughed him up. I felt powerful knowing that I was getting the upper hand, and in the knowledge that I would continue to get the upper hand with this guy. I did, and he never told the teacher.

"On one occasion I even enlisted the aid of my

younger sister. She phoned him and pretended to be from a local radio station. She told him that he had been selected as the winner of a contest. He actually believed he had won! The next day in school, after he had told people about it, I had my buddy humiliate him with the true story.

"Life was good those years."

Life was good for Roger; it was a sunny, ego-surging time of adulation and power. It wasn't so good for poor Evan. Whatever possessed a ten-year-old child to create such a hell? Whatever causes a bully to bully? There is something incomprehensible about this kind of attitude, this kind of contemptuous approach to another's pain. Even as adults we find it hard to understand how anyone can hurt another human being, let alone a hapless, helpless little child. And yet it happens, and it is because the

WHAT EXACTLY IS BULLYING?

If you peek through the fence at a typical school yard, you'll see what at first glance might seem like a pretty tough place, bubbling over with bruising scuffles and rough-and-tumble tussles. It may not look pleasant, but that doesn't mean it's bullying.

What makes it bullying is the element of power. When two kids of equal power scuffle in the school yard, it's just a fight—your average childhood jockeying for position. But when there's a power differential—a smaller, weaker child against a strong one, for example, or one child against a group of kids—that's when the adult alarm bells should go off: this is bullying and it's serious stuff.

It doesn't have to be a physical attack either. Name-calling, racial taunts, isolation, intimidation, destruction of property, stealing, extortion: if it involves repeated, malicious attempts to humiliate a helpless victim, if the victim is fearful, does not know how to make it stop, then it's bullying.

HOW OFTEN DOES BULLYING HAPPEN?

Most teachers agree that almost every child is subject to a bit of bullying at some point during his or her school days. The question is, how much? New research shows that the bully is a lot busier than we would like to think.

Dr. Dan Olweus has pioneered work in the field. In one of the world's first in-depth studies on bullying, he surveyed more than 150,000 students in Norway and Sweden and found that 9 per cent of the children in Grades 1 through 9 are fairly regular victims of bullying, and that 7 to 8 per cent of the students admit to bullying others.

There is some evidence that North American school yards may be a little rougher than their Norwegian counterparts. One Canadian study[1] found about half of all students said they had been bullied at least once during the term, and in another survey[2], three-quarters of the Canadian boys and girls said they had been picked on by their peers at least once. In the United States, researchers have found an alarming 80 per cent of middle school students surveyed had bullied someone during the last month[2a], and 80 to 90 per cent of adolescents report some form of victimization by bullies at school.[2b] Another American survey indicated 56 per cent of students knew of bullying that was happening in their schools, and one out of 10 students worried about being attacked (more elementary, middle and junior high school students than senior high). The most recent Canadian study, by Statistics Canada, found one in 20 boys and one in 14 girls is bothered by a bully.

Researchers say that, compared to youngsters in other countries, Canadian children are more aggressive in relationships with each other, pick on each other a little more and tend to be a little more dependent on their friends for guidance and support. They are also much more likely to be afraid of at least one of their fellow students, especially at age 11.

But there are bullies around the world. In fact, Cambridge psychological criminologist David P. Farrington, who has summarized the various pockets of research being done around the world, reports that in every country that has studied the problem the prevalence of bullying is quite high.

bully has problems too, many of them related to his home life and the way he was raised.

While we may not have a lot of sympathy for the bully, it might help to understand a little of what's going on in the brute's brain. In understanding his troubles, we may be less hell-bent on punishment or revenge. And when you consider the numbers, it's worth it. According to a recent Canadian study, one in seven boys and one in 11 girls between the ages of four and 11 are bullies.[4] And in the United States, researchers warn that schoolyard bullying is rampant, possible stoking anger among victims that can erupt in violence. A reported two-thirds of bully victims go unnoticed.[5]

But it's easy to get lost in the statistics, easy for the gritty playground pain to be dulled by numbers. Psychology professor Dr. Debra J. Pepler carried out a unique study that doesn't excise the emotion. Pepler and her researchers[6] strategically placed cameras in two average Toronto elementary-school playgrounds and hooked remote microphones up to several children at recess time to find out what was going on. What they recorded is a stinging view of a secret world.

A drama is unfolding before the camera: social justice, schoolyard style. "Mark" has made the big mistake of bumping another child. The school bully decides Mark needs to be taught a lesson. The bully marshals his troops: his "henchmen" are another girl and boy. Together they trap Mark at the top of the slide, surround him, pummel him. Mark is shouting, crying, "Stop kicking me you guys, ow. You're hurting me." From afar, this looks like a healthy recess activity, kids frolicking on the playground equipment. But the camera and the microphone reveal what's hidden: the boy is cornered and cowering. Finally Mark is saved by the ringing bell. Play time is over, but Mark's pain is not. The bullies have a mission; they'll save it for later. "We're going to kick your head in," they warn him as he huddles atop the monkey bars. "You're going to pay." They return to the classroom, supposedly to learn.

Watching this tape later, Debra Pepler shakes her head. It still disturbs her that children can be so cruel and that such cruelty goes unchecked. Pepler and her researchers had originally set out to tape aggression in kids. They were shocked at the amount of bullying going on and re-analyzed the tapes for types of bullying. Of the 52 hours of recorded tape, her researchers discovered an alarming 400 episodes of bullying, four of them involving knives.

That's a bullying every seven-and-a-half minutes.

And where were the teachers when all this was happening? They certainly weren't rushing to the students' rescue. In fact in only 4 per cent of the cases did they do anything at all. Part of the reason for their lack of involvement may be ignorance. They probably had no idea there was trouble afoot. It takes a skilled eye to detect childhood bullying. Many of the episodes recorded by Pepler are fleeting and subtle; the average length was 38 seconds. One painful recording, however, shows a boy being tormented by a group of bullies for 37 minutes—without adult assistance.

Who are these bullies who, careless and cavalier, tromp over others' pain? Bullies of the past used to be known troublemakers from troubled homes on the other side of the tracks. Today's bully knows no boundaries: he is male, female, urban or rural, rich or poor. She is the average kid next door. He is one of a group of friends. But researchers have come up with some common characteristics among childhood thugs.

THE "TYPICAL" BULLY

Children seem to have an innate sense of who a bully is and why. Ten-year-old Lisa has grappled with the problem and worked out her own stoic explanation:

"By hurting other people the bully can feel better about himself. Bullies usually pick on people who cry or complain when they are being bullied. Sometimes they bother people out of jealousy—for example if they're jealous of someone who has nicer hair than them, they bully so the jealousy doesn't show. Sometimes a child is raised thinking he is superior to other children and eventually they get so mean and bossy they become known as a bully. Other times, if someone tries to get revenge on a bully and is successful, he may do it more and more until he becomes a bully himself. So take my advice—there is no sure way to prevent bullies, but stay away from them anyway."

This child's-eye view of bullies appears to be pretty close to the mark. New research has painted a vivid picture of the average bully. He or she *probably* is

- strong, confident and impulsive;
- has low verbal intelligence and does not do well at school
- the same age or slightly older than his victims;
- aggressive with everyone: peers, parents, teachers and siblings;
- from a family that is neglecting, hostile or ineffective;
- a child whose father is aggressive and uninvolved;

- surrounded by a group of like-minded, easily swayed conspirators;
- not empathetic to his victims; shows no remorse;
- interested in bullying for the thrill, power and sense of control.

Some studies have put that old image of the big, dumb, insecure bully to rest. Quite often the bully comes across in surveys as surprisingly intelligent and self-assured, with little anxiety, average levels of insecurity and reasonable self-esteem. However, he may also have a disruptive, hyperactive personality and think violence is a swell way to solve problems.

This is someone who is not terribly likeable, not terribly pitiable—and yet nature and poor nurturing have left him firmly ensconced at the top of the schoolyard hierarchy.

THE DIFFERENCE BETWEEN MALE AND FEMALE BULLIES

"At the end of the eighth grade my parents decided I would benefit from a high-profile Catholic school in a wealthy area of town," a teenager recounts. "I was sent to this school not knowing a single person. My first day in English class started it all. Kevin was a boy in my class who sensed my insecurity and nervousness right from the start. He made up this rumor that I was a lesbian. From that day on, he and his friend taunted me, shoved me into lockers, tripped me in the halls, embarrassed me and kept me miserable. Teachers picked up on it and always punished them, which made it worse because they would make up some new rumor about me. One day I

went to school and found out they had been
suspended. It turned out that I hadn't been the
only girl who had been bullied by these boys. A
brave girl had reported them to the principal and
the boys were suspended for sexual harassment."

Childhood is an equal opportunity world, as far as bullying goes. Girls and boys both have a hand in it, and studies show they are equally aggressive—though it may
manifest itself in different ways. Girls have been known
to surround a male victim and beat him expertly and
savagely. And boys bullying girls—including ogling and
rumor-mongering—has long been an accepted part of
school life. I remember vividly the fear I felt in high
school when the lunch bell rang. I knew I would have to
pass the gym on the way to the cafeteria and face the
jocks who slumped against the radiators "rating" the girls
and making suggestive remarks. On occasion the male
gym teachers hung out there too with lewd grins of their
own. I sometimes opted to eat my lunch in the washroom
stall rather than face that gauntlet. It never occurred to
any of us girls that we had a right to complain. And yet
studies show that when ignored, and even subtly
condoned by school officials, this type of bullying can be
linked to date rape and domestic violence.

It is only recently that this type of bullying has earned
its own title: sexual harassment.

Both boys and girls find themselves the butt of the
bully's so-called jokes, but some studies show that boys
more often identify themselves as the pranksters. Boys
are more likely than girls to say they would join in a
bully's pranks. And boys are more likely to suggest striking back at a bully if they find themselves being attacked.

Girls, on the other hand, opt for avoidance and getting help from friends as the best plan of defence.

Much of the difference between the sexes can be attributed to society, and media in particular. Just look at the toys aimed at boys—action figures, games of militaristic might—and their favorite TV shows—*World Wrestling Federation*, *Beast Wars*, and the venerable *Batman*. The lesson is simple and scary: whether you're a good guy or a bad guy, guys use force to get their way. Girls, meanwhile, are socialized to hold back their anger and internalize their problems; if they are bullied, they are somehow at fault.

The gap between male and female physical bullying may be narrowing, in North America at least. In the last two decades the incidence of female bullying has risen dramatically. One international study found that girls in Canada are more likely to be picked on than girls in other countries. Police and school officials report female-perpetrated violence is becoming more frequent—and just as vicious as male violence. A study of Grade 9 girls in Ontario showed they were more likely than their male peers to say they would take another student's lunch money, beat up or threaten somebody with a weapon, or steal using threats of physical violence at school. In a second study, girls in Grades 6 to 8 were more likely than their male peers to report threatening another student or hurting others using a weapon.[7]

It's not certain why more girls are deciding to hit back. It may be because society is now telling them that they are just as good as the boys, equal in every way. They are taking that message literally, opting for the macho approach to relationships—the "You *Go* Girl!" attitude gone awry.

There are definite differences, however, between the way boys and girls bully. Boys who physically mature earlier than their peers tend not to be victimized, while the oppo-site is true of girls who mature earlier. When a boy is the bully, his assaults tend to be physical and direct. And the boy who gets the brunt of the bullying tends to be the one who avoids aggressive rough-and-tumble play. If you're a quiet little boy, for example, who loves puzzles and draw-ing pictures, the teachers may love you but the rest of the young male world probably doesn't. You don't fit into their clearly marked territories for boy and girl behavior.

Not a lot is known about female bullying because it is so covert. It is known that girls are less likely to get into a physical fight than boys. That doesn't mean they are not as aggressive; they are. Their aggression just takes on different forms. Girls tend to bully indirectly, by isolating their victims or assaulting them through teasing and verbal back-stabbing. And their bullying is less related to sex-stereotyped roles than boys' behavior; it more often has to do with social skills and appearance. Experts call it relational aggression. Boys value physical prowess and possessions most highly, thus their bullying takes on a more physical nature. Girls, on the other hand, value relationships, so girl bullies target relationships by spreading rumors, for example, to socially isolate the victim. In other words, they get 'em where it hurts.

Though the scars from this type of bullying aren't as visi-ble, they are there nonetheless. In fact, for most girls, social ostracism can hurt far more than a simple fist in the face. And because it's more subtle, female bullying may be more difficult for adults to detect and nearly impossible to erad-icate. Studies have found that teachers intervene more in physical bullying than in social bullying. The female victim is more likely to put up with this type of bullying silently because it is so important for girls to fit in. The alternative—to resign herself to being an outcast—may be more painful and more shattering to her self-esteem.

Among many male and female bullies there is a common characteristic: a history of aggressive behavior and parenting difficulties. The bully's roots run deep, starting in early childhood, building momentum as time goes on.

BULLYING AT DIFFERENT AGES

At age two, Jason was a hitter and a biter. Not unusual. Many toddlers are. But at age three, as his preschool companions eased up a bit on the aggression, Jason stepped up his attacks. Everything was a gun (sticks and spoons included) and he was always the bad guy. Mom was at a loss and Dad was proud of his little boy's "spunk." By four he was running the show at his day-care center. And by five, at his small school in the heart of the Prairies, his kindergarten teacher knew she had trouble on her hands.

The bully is at his prime in elementary school, but the warning signs can appear much earlier. Studies have shown that little tykes have individual differences in aggression as young as age three. Early on, some of these future bullies exhibit difficult temperaments and a tendency to resist their parents' control. But that doesn't neccessarily doom them to a lifetime of bullying.

Most toddlers seem "difficult" at some time or another, and behavior that resembles bullying—pushing, grabbing toys and so on—is common among preschoolers as they learn to socialize, share and figure out appropriate ways of getting what they want. This is not considered particularly worrisome or regarded as a prediction of things to come. Good parenting can usually tame the most turbu-lent toddler. By kindergarten, however, some children have not left this aggressiveness behind. For many, aggression is their way of adapting to a new environment and it goes away over time. For others, it's just a devel-opmental stage that they grow out of. But one study in Montreal found that aggressiveness sticks—and causes long-term trouble—among some of the boys, usually those growing up in troubled homes headed by young single mothers. Studies show that the bully's home may be one in which money is tight, conflict is frequent and the children probably attend day care.[8]

By the time they reach Grade 1 or 2, children will have mastered basic social skills. That's when you can often tell who is going to be the bully and who isn't. In fact, there are reports of gangs of bullies as early as Grade 1— and it is not uncommon now to find students in grades 1 or 2 committing serious acts of violence. In one case, a group of six- and seven-year-olds dominated their class, requiring other children to steal chocolate bars if they wanted to be allowed to join their "gang." Physical bullying behavior begins to peak during the elementary school years, especially among children who are in the highest grades.

Once the pattern is set, the misbehavior frequently intensifies as the bullies grow older. Children who were bullies at age 14 had already been rated as troublesome at age eight to ten by their peers and teachers, according to one study.[9] They had probably had sexual intercourse at an early age, had many delinquent friends and had committed many delinquent acts. It's important to note, however, that this aggressive behavior is not etched in stone: once a bully, not always a bully. As kids enter puberty, change friends or move to new schools, they may drop their role as bully and move into more normal relationships. A study of British schools found that bullying dropped from 35 per cent in the third year of school to 17 per cent in the seventh year.[10] But those who do continue their bullying up the ante as they age. They may be fewer in number, but they're meaner in spirit, moving on, quite often, to sexual harassment, date violence and aggression against society in general.[11]

Bullying also slinks under cover as children grow older. Among older children, bullying tends to be less physical and more social or verbal in nature.

One of the most worrying stages seems to occur in Grades 5 and 6, when children who were surveyed tended to blame the victim for his or her woes. Puberty is a prime time for bullies. Children are jockeying for status, crystallizing their morals and judgments and making mistakes that have much further-reaching implications than ever before. They are experimenting with relationships with the opposite sex, emotions and hormones are raging, society is pressuring them to hurry up and grow up and many youngsters find themselves in situations that are just too hot to handle.

Michael is in Grade 6, just 11 years old, but because he's tall he is often mistaken for 13. That's gone to his head. He tries to have a girlfriend the way the older, cool kids do. He tries to slip into their ranks. But he's out of his league and the others know it. They set him up, trick him into believing his girlfriend wants to break up with him. Finally Michael finds himself on the outside, barred from the clique, being kicked around by a bunch of girls. The girls know what they are doing; they aim their blows at the boy's most vulnerable parts. He tells his mom he's sick and doesn't want to go to school any more.

Teachers at the middle-school/junior-high level say they sometimes feel more like police officers than educators. One parent marvels at how much time her child's Grade 6 teacher spends resolving fights and drying up tears. Long after the work day ends, the teacher is still calling parents at home, trying to sort out the various messes.

This is the time when the bully just seems to gallop through the classroom ranks, he and his cavalry unchallenged and unrestrained. At this age, bullies say they bully because it's fun. They see their victims as weak-kneed wimps or nerds, too chicken to fight back. When they move to a new school, as they do in areas that have middle or junior high schools, many resort to bullying behavior to establish dominance among their new group of peers. Some believe being tough makes them popular. It probably does.

One Grade 6 bully remembers his childhood years with fondness, a kind of golden, untarnished reign of power and popularity. "I was a favorite of Miss Barnes, our teacher. I was also in the top 5 per cent of the class. All this combined to make me feel secure and immune from punishment."

Bullies aren't always who we think they are. Because they are often born leaders and masters at manipulation, teachers are often fooled. And the bullies often fool themselves too. They usually don't see themselves as bullies, but rather as popular and self-confident fellows who like a good laugh now and again.

THE BULLY'S SKEWED VIEW OF THE WORLD

Billy blames many of his problems on his hot temper. He doesn't think he is a bully. But "if someone bumps into me or something in the halls, I just fight." Some things really bug him, he says, and he responds with his fists. "I guess I don't have a very good temper any more. If I actually thought about it, I guess I wouldn't really want to fight. I just never think about it. I just do it."

For some reason, things that wouldn't bother other people really bother Billy. There are some experts who believe that bullies like Billy interpret social signals differently.

For example, if a child is standing in line at school and someone bumps him from behind, he may simply assume it was accidental and ignore it. But studies have shown that some kids will immediately believe the child who bumped him had malicious motivation, and will retaliate fast and furious. That characteristically negative way of interpreting social situations is constant and is set at an early age. Child development experts are examining early family behavior to see what causes it.

Researchers have found physically abused kids are most likely to have this negative interpretation of routine social interaction. By constantly expecting hostile actions from others, they find themselves in constant trouble. Dr. Kenneth Dodge, a professor of psychology at Vanderbilt University who is studying this phenomenon, calls it "hypervigilance."

Compared to their peers, these bullies can think up few solutions to problems other than violence. Typically, they jump to conclusions, they are often paranoid and they think others are trying to hurt them.

The sad irony is that such a child expects trouble,

Dodge says, and with the slightest provocation, will respond aggressively. Next thing he knows, he's got trouble, just as he expected. He fulfills his own prophesy because his response makes enemies and gives him the reputation for being a fighter. It's a reputation he must live up to.

While his happier classmates may be looking at life through rose-colored glasses, the bully has switched his shades for a much darker tint—and to him things look pretty bleak. It's a sort of social blindness that discolors his view of all relationships. Studies show bullies are more likely to believe their parents are rejecting them, their teachers are unfair, and other children are mean to them. Relationships, for this type of bully, are poisoned with anger, hostility and threats. His negativity causes other children to avoid him and in his isolation he acts out even more. Shunned by the mainstream, he finds a place among other anti-social children who reinforce his bad behavior. At the same time, the bully's hot-headedness leads him to seek high-risk activities for excitement. Adults interpret his behavior as belligerence and they become tense and stressed around him. This makes the situation even worse; it's hard to give lots of warm hugs and unconditional love to such a difficult child. Increasingly harsh punishment brings about more aggression. In a sense, the bully's temperament can ensnare him in a web of bad behavior.

Other bullies display aggression because they believe it's the most effective strategy in a social situation. This type of bully is goal-oriented and task-oriented and may tease others because she thinks it's the best way to impress her peers. In her mind, it has nothing to do with hurting others; it's simply a means to an end. The five-year-old may grab the ball from others because she thinks it's the most effective way of getting what she wants. Such a child is more likely to think aggression pays, and in a way it does: with increased self-esteem, control, respect. What's more, as her bad reputation grows, she is less and less likely to get into trouble because no one in the playground dares to tattle. Lots of positive feedback, very little negative.

Dodge believes that this behavior may originate in the home, where the child does not have a close relationship with any family member who can teach and model empathy. In fact many experts believe the home is the bully's breeding ground. What happens there, happens in the school yard.

THE BULLY'S FAMILY LIFE

Tommy's troubles ran like a hurricane through his family, leaving devastation in its wake.

His dad was always distant and showed more affection for his daughter. Tommy, who was a handful for any parent (he was later diagnosed as being hyperactive with an attention-deficit disorder), was raised almost entirely by his mom. The only attention he got from his dad was when Tommy beat up his sister—so he did. He could count on Dad to come running and really raise hell. At least it was some sort of attention.

To make matters worse, his puppy, his best buddy in the world, started becoming jealous of his younger sister. When the dog leapt up and bit her one day, the dog had to go. Tommy was devastated. His bullying got worse and worse until finally, when the children were both teenagers, he tried to kill his sister by smothering her with a pillow. Later that day she took an overdose of pills—and fortunately survived. His dad walked out the door for good. Tommy turned to beating up others, got into trouble with the law, abused his mother physically and verbally, and was sent to a foster home. Now that he is away from his home, he says he has finally come to grips with the fact that no matter how much of a fuss or furor he creates, his father will never be his friend.

While some children are bullies just because it makes them popular, others come from violent and stormy homes, ones in which parents—dads especially—are authoritarian, hostile, rejecting, negative or indifferent. Some studies show that bullies do not feel close to their parents and believe that their parents do not care for them.

Harsh, inconsistent discipline may be partially to blame. It's a case of too little love and too few limits. The child-rearing techniques employed by a bully's parents aren't neccessarily the best, and parents of a bully often

- tolerate aggressive behavior or even promote it;
- are more physically aggressive;
- don't monitor their children's whereabouts;
- have the television on more;
- fight among themselves more;
- are not aware of who their kids' friends are.

Mothers may lack self-confidence, fathers may be disrespectful of their wives. In fact, while everyone in the home plays a role in creating a bully, the father's role may be crucial. An abusive, uninvolved family hands a child the bully gun; the father's aggressive, unfriendly attitude is often the trigger. It's common for bullies to express negative attitudes towards their fathers and for the bullies' fathers to participate very little with them in leisure activities.

These are adults who have a poor understanding of the effects of physical punishment. They think spanking is fine, when in fact they are teaching their children that it's acceptable for a big person to hurt a little one. Their spanking is also injecting hostility into a relationship that should be building trust. That hostility and mistrust may find its way into the school yard.

Researchers have found many bullies' parents have a criminal record. Studies also show the majority of bullies don't attend church, and many come from large families. One study found bullies' parents tend to be poor, young, unemployed and under such stress that they inadvertently teach their children to be aggressive.[12] Another study carried out in Scotland found bullies often come from families in a lower socioeconomic class, have three or more siblings and tend to live apart from their natural parents.[13]

If the home is abusive, there's a good chance the child will be too. Men who have struck their wives, used physical punishment on their children or have been convicted of violent acts tend to have children who turn into bullies themselves. The children become locked in an unhealthy family tradition: teenage bullies grow up to be adult bullies who raise children to be bullies too.

Dr. Dan Olweus found four major factors that help create an aggressive personality problem:

- lack of warmth and involvement of the primary care-taker during the child's early years;
- permissiveness—the caretaker does not provide clear limits to aggressive behavior towards peers, siblings and adults;
- parenting is characterized by physical punishment and violent emotional outbursts;
- the child's individual temperament: some children appear to be born more aggressive or with more volatile emotions—they are more hot-headed and highly active.

Ironically, a bully's parents are often proud of her. After all, isn't she displaying the character traits we so admire—leadership, self-confidence, assertiveness? *My* child's not going to let anyone push *her* around. What spunk! What chutzpah! My fiery, feisty kid—a chip off the old block!

This may be a home that has gone overboard on teas-ing, sarcasm and criticism, and gone *under*board on humor, camaraderie, praise or interest.

Or it may be a home in which being rough and rugged is a survival skill. If it is a tough environment—a neigh-borhood that's not very safe, for example—parents will want the child to be tough too. Studies show that more aggressive kids often come from violent neighborhoods, and that the aggressiveness lingers, even if the child leaves for somewhere more civilized.

As one young gang member put it, "If you've been phys-ically abused you know how to physically abuse other people. You've been taught how to do it... and intimidate them in a way that they won't go to the police."[14]

Sibling relationships are another important area that

can make or break a bully. The love-hate roller coaster that all children ride with their brother or sister is jam-packed with lessons both on getting along and on standing up for themselves. Some sibling conflict is normal within most families. Things usually really heat up between the ages of six and 12. But when a child is regularly roughed up by a brother or sister—bullied physically or mentally—serious long-term problems can result.

It's not uncommon for a younger child who is bullied by an older sibling to take out his frustrations by bullying other children. It can also happen when an older child is left in charge of the younger ones. These pint-sized caregivers often use big-stick discipline. It's the only way they know of getting control, and younger children learn to model that inappropriate behavior in their own relationships.

With the increase in single mothers raising children and the decrease in the extended family, a young boy may be missing an appropriate male role model in his life. Researchers say some of these fatherless children may be left alone, unsupervised, while mother is out working. Among bored and uncontrolled children, whoever's bigger usually rules the roost.

And even among supposedly average parents—those who head up regular run-of-the-mill supportive and loving families—there's a worrisome trend that could contribute to bullying problems. Often when parents take their children to family-oriented activities, they prefer to stand aside and talk with their adult friends while their kids play among themselves some distance away. The parental absence means there's no immediate feedback for appropriate and inappropriate social behavior. The same applies to working parents who are too busy to know what their kids are up to. Children may be left to make up their own rules and codes of behavior.

The end result is often children raising children. A dangerous proposition. And the child who is being bullied, whether at home or in the playground, can quite easily turn around and bully others.

THE BULLY/VICTIM

> Lori was angry. A neighborhood girl was swearing at her, threatening her and following her home. So she got revenge. She bullied another girl who seemed to be afraid of her. Walking home from school she passed this girl walking in the opposite direction. "I maintained eye contact and I could see by her reaction—she was scared and nervous—that the bad eye worked." She did this whenever she saw the girl. Even though she knew nothing about the girl, it was thrilling to have someone else terrified of her. She found out later that her intimidating stares caused the girl incredible stress and regular nightmares. It made her feel lousy but it taught her a lesson and gave her some insight. Her bully, she discovered, had been bullied too, by a rough older brother. She says it taught her that the bully may sometimes be venting her own pain and frustration.

A good number of bullies may be doing just that—lashing out at someone else.

Children don't always fit into neat bully/victim categories. In fact it's not unusual for kids to take on both roles. Many bullies report that they have been victimized also; the bullying may be their attempt at self-defence. Perhaps surprisingly, studies have found that 45 per cent of children observed by researchers as either bully or victim were seen in both roles.[15] These are children whose lives are fraught with conflict and who are of most concern to child development experts. They are children who are rejected and unhappy—disruptive, irritating and unpopular with their peers. Sometimes this type of child is known as the shy-extrovert or counter-phobic personality. She is shy and scared and compensates with aggression. The aggression can earn her enemies and social isolation, which is just another form of victimization. It's a hard hole to climb out of.

A young girl is wandering through the playground, weaving among the clusters of children, conspicuous in her solitude. She trails behind a group of younger children, grabbing them, touching them and acting inappropriately. They do their best to avoid her.

The bully turns to a group of children her own age who are skipping. She tries to join in. The other girls tell her to get lost.

She tries, unsuccessfully, to enlist the recess monitor's help in getting the kids to play with her. A short while later you can hear her, out of the camera's sight, intimidating another child.

She then finds a new girl at the school who seems friendless and tries desperately to make her a friend: grabbing her coat, begging her, ordering her not to leave. Finally the new girl complies, saying, "First, if you want to be in my club forever, put out your arm." The girl does. The new girl says, "This is going to hurt but I have to do it." She scrapes the bully/victim's arm with a pocket knife.

Often a bully will harass other children to force them to join in the bullying. Here, the bully's assistants are victims too. These bully/victims find themselves unwittingly using violence on their peers in self-protection and fear: the "better-him-than-me" mind set.

"I enlisted the aid of another guy, Wayne, to help me harass my victim." Rob describes his glory days as the school bully. "Wayne was slow-witted and easy to manipulate. I had a back-up plan that if Wayne ever implicated me I'd deny everything." That never happened. Wayne stood by him all the way. He was too afraid not to.

The bully/victim is not the only one on the bully's team. Anyone who has ever had a bout with the bully can testify to the fact that the villain is rarely in on it alone. Invariably there are others, either as an audience egging him on or as opportunistic accomplices waiting for their chance to join the fun and throw a few blows of their own. There are some who speculate that if it weren't for the bully's cheerleading team, there wouldn't be bullies at all. Peer pressure crowns the bully king or queen of the school yard. Peer pressure keeps him there.

THE POWER OF PEER PRESSURE

I remember one boy named Stuart Baron. He was quiet and didn't have a lot of friends. But his main failing was that he cried easily. I was one of several girls who grabbed at that weakness and rubbed it in his face. We'd circle and taunt him at recess: "Baby Baron, Baby Baron, Baby Baron gonna cry." We'd sing this at his face until he did cry. Then we'd laugh. It's so strange. Individually, we were all nice girls from nice homes. The teachers liked us because we were good kids. But when we got together over this one kid, something happened. The devil took hold.

Mob mentality slips subtly, easily, into schoolyard play. These girls wouldn't dream of cruelty on their own. But peer pressure and peer presence can easily lead a weak-willed child down the wrong path. Not a lot is known about the role of peers in maintaining and exacerbating bullying. But there is little doubt their role is a big one.

Bullying relies on an audience. Filming of playgrounds shows that the vast majority of the time, other children are watching the bullying, excitedly jumping, yelling and pumping up the action. Police have noticed an increase in youth violence during the school year and a dramatic decline during holidays or school strikes. After all, what's the point if there's no one to impress?

Although peers are close by to witness or take part in most cases of bullying, they rarely intervene. And when they do step in, it seldom does much good.

They are clustered by the baseball diamond. A large boy has found a target: one of the smaller boys hovering nearby. The bully knocks him around a bit, then grabs another boy and bullies him into fighting the smaller one. "Come on, don't be scared," he taunts the apprentice bully. "I'll protect you if you want to fight him."

The smaller child is knocked to the ground and a group of boys swarm around, shouting, "Kick him in the seed, get him. He's on the ground, come on, go get him now." A few children, brave observers, try to stop this: "Leave him alone, ease up already." They are ignored. Much later, when the school bell signals the return to class, he is huddled up against a corner of the fence, alone.

You have to admire the little ones who tried to stop such an episode. It must have taken a real internal battle to provoke them to speak out and risk their own hides. The action of the other boys, who were intimidated into joining the violence, is much more common.

Even though the vast majority of children really don't like bullying, kids find themselves joining in anyway. According to one study, an alarming 33 per cent reported they would join in.[16]

The bully's popularity is a puzzle. How can he hold such sway over them all? Surveys show bullies are generally not well-liked by other students. They are not the kind of friend the other kids want to play with, yet they're often the center of activity just the same, and are frequently nominated by their peers as leaders.

Schools have definite pecking orders. Children quickly learn to get on the bully's side for survival. Joining a bully is a form of self-preservation. And by joining his league, the corroborators get the added benefit of a sense of superiority over someone else, living by that age-old dictum: build yourself up by putting somebody else down. In addition, children sometimes believe the only people who understand them are other children, so they do what they must to gain their respect, even though it means risking adults' wrath and violating their own rickety moral code.

I remember how we used to tease the Brown kids. We were all children from relatively well-to-do homes and the Browns (there were three girls) lived in a shack near the creek. Their house always looked a mess. Their hair was never combed, they wore weird clothes, they were extremely shy and not too intelligent. One of the girls was in the class for slow learners. They would huddle together at the front of the school bus and the louder kids would make rude remarks about them, saying "Ooh, you touched a Brown. Now you've got cooties." Or pointing to imaginary lice in their hair. I felt so sorry for them. I knew it wasn't fair. What did they do wrong to deserve this?

Once I even did the brave thing of sitting beside one of the girls and being nice. I felt so noble. That was when none of the loud kids were around. But when the bullying was going on, I'm ashamed to say, I laughed along with them, because I was afraid. I was shy too and I didn't want to get lumped in with the Browns. Towards the end of elementary school one of the younger Brown girls drowned in the creek. The newspaper photo showed her little footprints in the snow leading out to a hole in the ice. She'd wandered out in the middle of the night and they didn't discover her until morning. I think the entire school was chastened by that event. I probably wasn't the only one to cry buckets for that lost soul. After that, no one bullied the Browns any more.

It's so easy for gullible, vulnerable children to be sucked into a whirlpool of cruelty. Dr. Olweus blames it on four developmental learning processes:

- social contagion: people tend to behave more aggressively after watching others behave aggressively. Kids may join in to boost their prestige and acceptance.
- weakening of inhibitions: there are few negative consequences for bullies, lots of rewards. Because he gets away with it, others are encouraged to try.
- diffusion of responsibility: within a group, there's less likelihood of guilt, remorse or responsibility.
- reputation: bullies may develop a reputation as one to seek out when in need of strength or protection, while the victim comes to be seen as one who deserves the abuse.

That's why it seldom works to try and stop the bully on an individual basis after the children enter school. There is too much reinforcement by the bully's peers. One-on-one mediation won't work because *everyone* is involved. It has to be across-the-board.

That's also why bullies continue to get away with it. It takes a very brave child to step away from the crowd. It's not always easy, or fruitful, to intervene. A 14-year-old high-school student discovered this the hard way recently. He tried to help a 15-year-old friend who was being harassed by a bully. They were in the school yard and the bully was trying to set fire to the 15-year-old's hair. The 14-year-old happened to be standing nearby and tried to stop him, but the bully head-butted him, sending him to hospital. It was a powerful, unfortunate lesson for everyone.

Children are incredibly skillful at covering up bullying. Have you ever noticed the way a group of bullying children will flee the minute an adult face appears? It's part of the peer code that, whatever happens, whatever you do, don't let the adults know because they won't approve. Often the victim joins the cover-up, downplaying the experience because it's not cool to be the victim, or staying quiet in natural shyness or sheer terror while the fast-talking bully spins a tale to get the victim into trouble too.

When children get older, this protective shell can become impossible to crack. All those lone bullies and their henchmen congeal into big, intimidating groups; they have learned there's strength in numbers. Other youngsters have learned that if you can't beat them, you join them. The "swarm" is born. And the fear and power behind the big, bulky, bullying mob—the older child's version of the schoolyard bully—can form a frustrating fortress against parents, teachers and police.

THE OLDER BULLY

This was supposed to be Lauren's year to be "sweet 16." Instead, she's a scared senseless 16. That's because she recently made the big mistake of going out with the wrong boy. Turns out this guy was also seeing another girl with a powerful group of friends. They ambushed her one day when she ventured into their neighborhood in her small Northern Ontario town, and they taught her a lesson, one that involved bruises, scrapes, a black eye and a broken arm. Lauren isn't seeing anyone now. In fact she spends most of her time in her bedroom. The girls warned her they'd kill her if

they saw her near their school again, and she
believes it. And no, of course she didn't press
charges. She says she didn't want to be a tattletale.

The change to group bullying can happen between the ages of ten and 14. Children become obsessed with impressing their peers. The bully with a face and identity disappears into the crowd. And the crowd adopts the bully attitude, becoming intoxicated with its own strength and prestige. Look, here's how to get your way, get a thrill and get away with it too!

These new group bullies are often average students who get their strength in numbers. They may not like your baseball cap or shoes. Maybe you dated the wrong guy. Maybe you dared "diss" someone—a teenager's word for a disparaging look. The reason is irrelevant. It's just an excuse to bash your head in. In some cities they call it swarming, elsewhere they call it curb stomping. In reality, it is bullying.

And in some cases, it can lead to tragic results. In a suburb of Victoria, British Columbia, recently, a 14-year-old girl found herself in a nightmare of teenage tormenting that ended when she was beaten and drowned. For a young girl, Reena Virk shouldered a heavy load: she was of a minority ethnic background, her family followed a strict Jehovah's Witness faith, she was heavy and tall for her age. For that, and for the professed reason that she "stole" another girl's boyfriend and spread rumors, a group of teens beat her so badly that she suffered 18 kicks to the head, stomping injuries to her back and chest and her internal tissues were crushed between her abdominal wall and her backbone. It started when one girl stubbed out a lit cigarette on her forehead. When she tried to flee, she was surrounded by a group of six girls who punched and kicked her until she sat slumped in the mud. A teenage boy came upon the scene and even though he did not know Virk, he kicked, punched and helped drown the Grade 9 student. Pathologists said Reena Virk would have died from head injuries if she hadn't drowned first.

Police and educators agree: this type of bullying in bulk is becoming more and more common, and at younger and younger ages. The old one-on-one confrontation is passé. Many youngsters today gather friends around them like a coat of armor. Companions act as tools of protection or ostracism or revenge. A group of friends becomes one great big, faceless bully.

These teenagers may take the group bully concept to a different level, using their power to trash parties, harass shopkeepers and tyrannize the weaker wherever they find them. And (what a thrill) they may even make it into the newspapers! In small towns and big cities, the new gang's antics are making news.

Police say these gangs are not Hell's Angels or romantic *West Side Story* characters, they're not members of any organized-crime gang—they're the boy and girl next door. It's hard to imagine an average individual kid out in the street rolling somebody, but it's as if they lose their identity when they're in a group.

"There's no peer pressure," one boy explains. "You don't get teased or called 'chicken' if you don't join in the bullying. It never gets to that point. If someone in the group says to do it, you just do and there's no thought."

But there *is* peer pressure. It's just a lot more subtle.

Three of Jan's four kids have been bullies or been bullied and she thinks her experience is typical of many families today. As one son said, "Either you take the bullying or you join in."

"Kids honestly don't think we adults can do anything about it," says Jan. "They say in the end it comes down to my friends against his friends."

Police say teens often tell them: "If we told our parents, they could get hurt." Youth count on their own ability to protect themselves because they don't believe their parents can. Mom and dad are just are too naive about this new world, this new breed of bully.

One young man says he and his friends beat up other people "because it gives us a rush, a sense of power." He looks upon it as a way of dealing with feelings of despair and helplessness. They swarm not for a trendy jacket but for a sense of control.

The group bully movement started in the late 1980s when kids became highly concerned about their appearance. Teenagers have always cared what they looked like, but this generation seemed to take it to an extreme. There is no way they would be seen carrying their lunch to school in a grocery-store shopping bag. And they wouldn't be caught dead buying running shoes in a regular department store. Status is something you buy, with lots and lots of money.

Middle-income kids bond over their music and clothes. The result is a school divided and grouped according to fashion and style. There are no longer just the preppies, nerds and stoners. Today's schools are a nest of cliques—goths, gangbangers, surfers, ravers, skaters, b-boys and kickers—an endless variety of self-styled loosely knit clubs—each tailored to their interests and localities, some more popular than others. In many schools, the inveterate jocks and cheerleaders remain ensconced at the top, flinging out abuse at the outcasts and misfits on the Doc Marten/black make-up/fringe fashioned sidelines.

Leadership in these gangs-cum-friendships is transitory. Whoever is the current manipulator of the group is at the helm. Unlike the old-fashioned stereotypical gangs, school is the group's main social focus because it is the magnet that brought them together in the first place; expanding suburbia means these youngsters are spread out all over the map and when school is out the gang is fragmented. Drugs are not usually an issue, and the crime is for fun, not profit. It's not easy to avoid the bully when he is no longer one but many; when he is no longer waiting for the victim by the back fence but roaming the street in toxic clumps, looking for someone to trash. They don't care much about getting caught because they believe their numbers make them untouchable. They're often right.

Typically, there are 15 group members to one victim. It's common to find gangs charging a dollar to use the washroom ("a loonie for the loo") and, if students are caught using the facilities without paying the toilet tax, they are beaten up. Sometimes, even if they do pay, they're beaten up anyway.

And just like the bully at a younger age, when gangs are successful at their intimidation, they're encouraged to do more. If they get the jacket or the hat, they feel empowered. They may be more likely to move from threats to pushing to inflicting injury.

In some areas, children of similar cultural backgrounds band together against racial taunts, forming a defensive wall against bullies. But if they settle scores in a violent way, they then become bullies themselves. And since there is no personal responsibility in a group, the bullying snowballs.

Police, parents and teachers are stymied because they can't persuade children to report the problem immediately. Young people just don't have faith in the adult world any more; they get their friends to handle things, forming vigilante groups to seek revenge on other groups of bullies. They begin power-tripping and the problem mushrooms.

HOW TODAY'S BULLYING HAS CHANGED

The old no-brain bruiser with the scrubby clothes and gap-toothed leer may have gone the way of the hickory stick; even the label "bully" is a little old-fashioned. But the bully is still out there stirring up the school yard. The nature of bullying has changed however and should concern us more than ever. It is more complicated, more aggressive and more severe. Kids move from aggressive feelings to aggressive behavior with lightning speed. We are witnessing a boom in pint-sized aggression, a more sophisticated, dangerous kind. And it scares parents.

They have good reason to be concerned. Educators, police and child experts have noticed bullying at the turn of the millennium is different; the stakes are higher. Today's kids are growing up in an angry, fast-paced, media-saturated, economically and ecologically unstable world, and their bullying seems to be crueler, nastier, more callous. It's certainly more sophisticated and no longer one-on-one. Remember the weight-lifting ads in the back of comic books, the ones that were supposed to help the poor sods who got sand kicked in their faces? The best way to get back at a bully, the ads maintained, was to build up a good set of muscles. Today kids build up an arsenal. Or a group of friends. Or are simply prepared to grin and bear it.

One mother laments the vanished days of her own youth. "Here we were, peace-loving hippies, making love not war and all that," she says, bewildered by the fact that her 16-year-old son is considered a bully. "It's such a contrast to these kids who have short hair, even shaved heads, and violence is something they really adore. The guy who turns up at school with a gun or knife, the mean looking guy, is the popular one, the one with all the clout."

More and more police are discovering guns, knives and clubs in school lockers. Kids don't flash muscles any more; they flash their knives. In many schools, a weapon is the ticket to popularity. Joe, 14, rattles off a list of the weapons kids brandish: "from an 'Uzi' to a finger nail file and (everything) in between. You've got guns, knives, swords, smoke bombs, chains, bicycle chains, lead pipes, wires, pool balls, shot put balls, whips." [17]

In a study funded by the National Institute for Justice, nearly three of every 10 high school boys in the United States reportedly has a gun, and half of the young people surveyed believe they can get firearms relatively easily. [18] In Canada, a *Toronto Star* survey of 1,019 Grade 10 students in the Metro Toronto area found 13 per cent of respondents said they brought a weapon to school in the past year, and almost half had seen another student at their school with a weapon.

Students surveyed said they armed themselves for self-defence. One parent from a quiet suburban neighborhood says her child's elementary school did a "locker sweep" and turned up 15 pellet guns. In some schools 40 per cent of students admit they carry knives for protection. Others use replica handguns and dangerous air pistols.

There is still a great deal of controversy, however, over whether young people are committing more violent crime today. Statistics in Canada and the United States indicate youth crime in general may have leveled off or dropped slightly in recent years, but it is still up from a decade earlier. Some criminologists say the rise is due to an increased reporting of minor crimes that used to be ignored by schools. The media is also giving criminal activity a higher profile. But many police like Brian O'Connor, a sergeant with Metro Toronto Police Youth Programs, call that "ivory tower talk." "When you're actually out there you know what's going on. There are a lot more disruptive kids in the classroom," he says. "It may not be criminal behavior, but there is a general discontent...a willingness to use weapons and the beatings are more severe."

Those who work with youth say crimes may actually be *under*-reported today because people have given up, police have decided the offenses are not worth charging, or because alternative measures, like mediation or counseling, are being pursued. Among criminologists, police and social workers, the issue has become intensely politicized and polarized. Reverend Fred Mathews, of Central Toronto Youth Services, believes it doesn't matter whether the numbers are up or down; what matters is that we are working to solve it. Mathews suggests community leaders gather official and anecdotal statistics, talk to kids, adults who work with kids, and social scientists, then, setting aside battles between academics and grassroots over turf and egos, have a serious, civil conversation to try to heal our society.

Those on the front line would welcome the change. Teachers say they can't help but notice an increase in violence in their own classrooms. Even preschool teachers have noticed the increasing rage, reporting a tendency among very young children to be slow to bond and quick to explode.

Kids are feeling threatened and intimidated at school. There's more foul language and harassment of other students at younger ages, children bristle more easily at perceived slights, use friends to settle scores through violence and build fledgling relationships on macho posturing. And at the recent hearings by the Ontario Royal Commission on Learning, the problem of violence in the schools was raised more than any other issue.

THE SIGNS OF A TROUBLED CHILD

- lack of interest in school
- absence of age-appropriate anger control skills
- seeing self as always the victim
- persistent disregard for or refusal to follow rules
- cruelty to pets or other animals
- artwork or writing that is bleak or violent or that depicts isolation or anger
- talking constantly about weapons or violence
- talking about bringing weapons to school
- obsessions with things like violent games and TV shows
- depression or mood swings
- bringing a weapon (any weapon) to school
- history of bullying
- misplaced or unwarranted jealousy
- involvement with or interest in gangs
- self-isolation from family and friends

The more of these signs you see, the greater the chance that the child needs help. If it's your child, try to discuss it with him or get a relative, teacher, counselor, religious leader or coach to broach the problem. If it's not your child but you know him well enough, express your concern to his parents. If they seem disinterested, speak to the child's teacher.[19]

"I remember being bullied when I was in Grade 8 or 9, but all it took was a trip by my parents to the principal and it was over with," one parent of teenagers remembers. "The thing we've been grappling with as far as our own kids are concerned is their total lack of respect for authority. They just don't care."

As one boy said to his mother as she cut into his cake celebrating his 16th birthday, "Now that I'm 16, I guess I can't break the law any more." He was serious; he'd just realized how careful he'd have to be in the way he bullied in the future. He'd better not get caught.

Police are frustrated. They are tired of an attitude they see among children that says if you want something, you take it, and to take it, you use force: intimidation, threats or assault. Some kids go through the entire school year without eating lunch because they've been handing over their lunch money for "protection" from school bullies.

The scene is a typical classroom corridor. Students rough-house and bumble along the halls, bang noisily into lockers, bump heavily into each other on the way to class. A teacher making her way through the antics gets banged up too. No one apologizes. Later, in the same school, a boy carelessly tilts back in his chair, snagging the teacher's nylons. Again, no apology. When the teacher comments, the boy tosses out a rough "Sorry" like peanuts to a monkey and a few classmates snicker.

One school principal says children don't show the same remorse when they do something wrong as did previous generations. They don't realize they've been mean, she says, and they're almost surprised when you inform them that they have.

School administrators say they are now seeing violence used by children more often as a way of dealing with difficulties, rather than discussion. Name-calling moves quickly to fighting, and it's much more vicious than a simple punch in the eye—sometimes impulsive, often coolly premeditated. Today's bullies have adapted to their harsh new world, still terrorizing weaker kids but in a more worldly, worrisome way.

WHY TODAY'S BULLIES ARE DIFFERENT

Why is this happening to our children? Why does the bully seem to be getting the upper hand in schools today?

Part of it may be that we're talking about bullying more than we ever did in the past as we become more concerned about human rights in general and as we empty our collective closets of other nasty secrets like racism, incest and domestic violence.

Some people point to an increase in all forms of aggression throughout society; the availability of handguns and weapons has made this increase a much more serious concern. Still others blame it on a combination of family breakdown, racism, poverty and unemployment.

Because families are busier than ever, it's tough to keep tabs on where the kids are. Police say that when they call home to tell parents about a child's violent behavior, the parents are often shocked. In this fast-paced world of multiple careers and multiple interests, it's not easy knowing what your kids are up to. And once they reach the babysitting age, 11 or 12, children are given more freedom and looser boundaries. The result is kids being left to make a lot of decisions on their own. Latchkey children are coming home to empty houses, being raised by older siblings and learning to fend for themselves. They develop a hard, tough veneer and learn about the survival of the fittest. They learn the bully's credo.

Family instability may be another important factor. When a family breaks up, the source of authority may be disrupted along with the family rules for good citizenship and behavior. In a thought-provoking essay on family breakdown in the *Atlantic Monthly*, April 1993, Barbara Dafoe Whitehead wrote of the situation in the United States:

> *Nationally more than 70 per cent of all juveniles in state reform institutions come from fatherless homes. A number of scholarly studies find that, even after the groups of subjects are controlled for income, boys from single-mother homes are significantly more likely than others to commit crimes and to wind up in the juvenile justice court, and penitentiary systems.... Principals report a dramatic rise in the aggressive acting-out behavior characteristic of children, especially boys, who are living in single-parent families. The discipline problems in today's suburban schools—assaults on teachers, unprovoked attacks on other students, screaming outbursts in class—outstrip the problems that were evident in the toughest city schools a generation ago. Moreover, teachers find many children emotionally distracted ... upset and preoccupied by the explosive drama of their own family lives.*[20]

Teachers are surprised at how poorly children handle anger, settle arguments, get along with others. These are skills we used to assume were being taught at home. Not any more. There's a new emotional illiteracy among the young generation. Kids don't seem to be able to read, or safely express, their own emotions. Nor are they sure of their own moral code. Surveys reveal today's youth are more likely to be influenced by their peers, the media, movies and popular music than by religious leaders. Values such as honesty, forgiveness and generosity are on the decline among young people, replaced with a belief system based on freedom and individual success.

*   *   *

From the old-fashioned, gum-chomping, big-muscled bully of yore to the new-style, armed, anonymous group bully, things have changed but they've really stayed the same. The bully is still out there causing trouble, thanks to poor parenting, peer pressure and a world that loves a fighter.

It is an overwhelming task to try to eliminate such an inveterate character as the schoolyard bully. But with commitment and unity, parents, children, teachers and the community can make a difference. The bully can be redeemed, with love and effort, shaped into a youngster who can use his natural leadership for society's good. It's up to all of us to help the bully. The next chapter shows how.

3

Helping the Bully

School buses seem custom-made for bullies and their pranks: a group of children of varying ages and abilities lumped together, day after day, in cramped little seats far from the prying eyes of adults, the bus driver way up front, too busy with the road to worry about discipline. John remembers those days. He was a bus driver in rural Ontario, and Donny was the thorn in his side. No matter what he did, the kid would not stop picking on the little ones. Reprimands didn't work. Neither did warnings. John tried seating Donny next to him, but when John's eyes were on the road, Donny was up to his tricks again.

Finally John noticed a group of older boys at the back who were also getting annoyed with Donny. When Donny did it again, he gave the boys the signal and they gently but firmly placed him outside the bus in a snow bank. Then slowly John moved the bus ahead. Donny ran alongside, pounding on the door. John stopped the bus and let him back in. Donny stormed up the steps, glared at the other kids (who were doing their best to suppress their giggles) and finally burst into laughter himself. It was the turning point, and from then on he was John's biggest helper, defrosting windows and throwing sand on the steps. "I'm not saying this is the best thing to do, I just know I had to do something dramatic ... not to get revenge or hurt him but to break through the dance we were doing. It happened to be the right thing at the time."

If you want to stop a bully, you can't do it off in a corner somewhere away from the rest of the world. You've got to include the bully's world or it just won't work. This is why John's approach did the trick: he had a ready-made captive audience. He could stop the bully in his tracks and make sure that everyone else *saw* that he was stopped. His particular approach—that of shaming the bully—may not have been as compassionate as it should have been, but making use of a captive audience and a sense of humor can prove highly successful.

Bullying is a community activity. Whether it is the school community, the neighborhood community, the school-bus community or the community of the family, bullying does not succeed in isolation. That's why the entire community must be involved in the solution. Your heart may not go out to him, but the bully needs help too, and in light of our increasingly violent society, defusing the bully may be best for us all.

Because so much bullying revolves around peer pressure and reputation, successful intervention should include everyone: parents, school, other children, the community and the bully himself. What follows are a few tips on taming the tyrant, beginning with the most important influences, the parents.

WARNING SIGNS—IS YOUR CHILD A BULLY?

The following are possible signs that your child may have a bullying problem:

- marks suddenly plummet.
- complains of being treated poorly by teachers or other kids.
- commits acts of violence to the family pet.
- engages in conflicts that lead to violence with siblings or with parents.
- associates with friends who seem to endorse violence (you might hear them laughing on the phone over some altercation, for example).

If you observe any of these signs, sit down and verify them first before jumping to conclusions. (This is why it's so important to establish good communication with your child right from the start.) Then explore with your child how he or she feels about what you've observed. Finally talk to him or her about what can be done about the problem. If the direct approach doesn't work, it may be a good idea to enlist a third party—a teacher or school counsellor—for their trained, unbiased viewpoint.

THE PARENTS' ROLE: HOW NOT TO RAISE A BULLY

Tom, a teacher, was frustrated and fed up. No matter what he did, Sam the bully continued to terrorize the elementary-school children. Finally Tom telephoned Sam's parents. The boy's mother answered the phone. The minute she learned what the call was all about, she put her husband on the line. "Oh, that," the dad said. "Just smack him on the head. Give him a kick in the butt. That'll straighten him out." Tom sighed. This was going to be an uphill battle. At least he knew now why Sam was the way he was.

Bullies are not born; they're created. Nature may have a hand in it—the child may have been born with a biological deficiency, hyperactivity, attention deficit disorder or a very reactive neurological system, for example—but it's how the parents manage that individual child and his biological baggage that determines the final outcome. And if things get off track, parents have the best chance at setting things straight again. Unfortunately, it's not always that easy. If the bully's parents have troubles of their own, and if their child-rearing skills aren't great, then they probably don't realize there's a problem at all. Usually, it goes unnoticed until someone connected with the victim speaks out.

It's one of those emotionally charged TV talk shows where the guests bare their souls and the audience vents its indignation. This one is on bullies. A victim has just told her sad story of childhood torment. Then the bully strides on stage, one hand placed nonchalantly in the pocket of his leather jacket, a sly grin slicing his face. As the audience berates him, his grin and his macho pride never falter. After all, he shrugs, she was only ten years old at the time. She's grown up now. Get over it already! It's obvious this chap has never got the message that being a tough guy is not acceptable.

Some experts believe that once the child reaches elementary-school age, aggressive behavior is so entrenched that it's almost too late to change it. Rehabilitation programs at the school level have not been terribly successful for that reason. Prevention is therefore the best medicine. Ideally, it begins at pregnancy, with preventative programs that can identify the high-risk children yet to be born. According to the experts, children born to mothers who are young, single and poor are at the greatest risk of becoming bullies. But there are few such preventative programs in existence yet. The next best approach is to help parents deal with their young at-risk children before bad habits are learned. That's because studies show early patterns of behavior are set or "hard-wired" into the brain during the first few years of life and may be impossible to unlearn later. The earlier a preventative program starts, therefore, the better its chances of success.

HOW TO SPOT A TOO-AGGRESSIVE PRE-SCHOOLER

The following behavior should set off some warning bells:
- intentionally breaks toys.
- provokes or annoys other people on purpose.
- displays a lack of empathy or conscience.
- hurts animals.
- hurts others, throws objects when upset.

If you are concerned, speak to a teacher or professional to find out if your concern is justified and to help your child learn more gentle behavior while he is still young.

How a parent deals with the child in his or her early years is crucial. And experts say that how parents handle discipline may be one of the most important issues. Here are some suggestions for helping an aggressive child—a potential bully—to get a grip before it's too late.

- Rules for good behavior should be made in advance,

when everything (and everyone) is quiet. It may help to write the rules down so that, when something happens and everyone is upset, there's an objective set of guidelines to call upon. It will seem more like a logical consequence, less like mom or dad trying to get even.

- When the child fails to live up to the agreed-upon standards of behavior, discipline should be as consistent as possible—and non-violent. A discipline approach that relies on physical punishment could lead to a whole host of other problems. The best approach is to use praise for good behavior, time-out or withdrawal of privileges for bad.

- The message that aggression is definitely not appropriate behavior should go out early and often. Parents should impress upon their children that toughness doesn't imply strength, and that hurting others is abhorrent.

- Be aware of the conflicting messages with which society bombards children—especially boys— regarding macho behavior. Do your best to ease his angst by accepting "non-macho" behavior—tears, gentleness—and by pointing out to him society's macho myths.

- Try to weave lessons on social rules and values throughout the child's early playtime experiences. Whenever conflict erupts, give clear guidance and expectations. It is wrong to hit, or, you don't take what doesn't belong to you, for example. Or help your child to include another child who is feeling left out.

- Reward your child's acts of kindness—when he shares or compliments another, for example.

- When he acts aggressively with other children, don't say you're upset with him. Rather, tell him you're upset with what he did and ask him about better ways he could have handled his feelings. Give him suggestions—walk away and ignore the problem, for example, or count to ten to allow the feelings to fade.
- For younger children, telling stories or drawing pictures may initiate a discussion about bullying and right and wrong behavior. Or try role-playing. Imagine situations in which children are uncertain how to behave, like sharing, name-calling or playing with a group. Together, act out the correct and incorrect responses and ask how the child feels in each situation.

ONE APPROACH TO PREVENTING BULLYING

The staff at Earlscourt Child and Family Centre in Toronto suggest this response to kids with aggressive tendencies: snap your fingers and count to ten whenever you feel trouble brewing. The snap stands for S.N.A.P.—Stop Now And Plan. This gives the aggressors time to think about what will happen if they bully and what will happen if they don't.

HOW SELF-ESTEEM PREVENTS BULLYING

Billy was one of those beautiful little boys who are often mistaken for girls. Fragile, with blond hair, he was such a nice kid, his mom remembers. But he had a learning disability and in Grade 3 he failed a grade. He no longer fit in and he felt like a failure. He was tormented terribly, coming home daily with bruises and black eyes. He pleaded with his mom not to talk to the school administrators about the bullying because the bullies would only beat him up worse for being a tattletale.

Eventually Billy discovered that if he acted brave and macho, that if he mouthed off to the teacher and skipped classes, the kids wouldn't pick on him so much. "Next thing you know he came home with his head shaved," his mom says. By 12 he had found new friends and they all took turns shaving each other's head. It wasn't a big step to becoming a bully himself. He was hanging out with 16-year-olds, beating up other children. One day his mom was floored to discover a jagged knife hidden in his bedroom. Since then he's been charged with possessing a stolen Chicago Bulls jacket and being involved in a gun fight. The arrests simply made him more popular. The gentle boy who wrote beautiful poetry and loved art and classical music is still there, but he's buried deep beneath the bully masquerade.

Between Grades 5 and 8, children are extremely vulnerable to peer pressure. If their self-esteem is on shaky ground, then it's not unusual for them to topple into the wrong crowd. This is why it's so important for parents to be aware of what their child is doing outside the home, who her friends are and if possible who her friends' parents are.

An otherwise well-behaved child who is easily swayed can quickly be sucked into a bully's schemes or into a group of bullies that likes to swarm for kicks. Strong self-esteem may be the best self-defence. A healthy sense of self-worth can go a long way towards making a child able to stand firm in the buffeting winds of peer pressure.

Here are ways parents can boost their children's self-esteem:

- It's important to listen to your child, to let him express his feelings verbally. Let him know it's all right to feel a full range of emotions. By taking the time to listen to his thoughts, you're teaching him not to repress negative feelings and let the hostility out at a later time, in a more destructive way.
- When you see your child respond with anger to a situation, let her know it's okay to feel angry, but it's not okay to act on those feelings by hurting someone else.
- Spend time with your child and treat him with respect. When discussing homework, for example, work out beforehand the ground rules. If he agrees to forgo all phone calls during homework time and you promise to take any messages, you will be modelling the behavior of mutually respectful adults.
- Help her find something good about herself, a talent that she can build upon and that will give her an identity other than class bully. Organized sports activities can help a lot because they can increase self-esteem, teach children how to live with rules and show them how to express aggression in a healthy way.
- Spend at least one hour of "quality" time with your children each day, cooking together, doing crafts, skating or playing in the park. Use this time to teach them about sharing, generosity, taking turns and communicating in healthy ways.
- Provide lots of opportunities for your child to experience both success and failure. Help him find

friends that bring out the best in him, and encourage lots of good socializing. Well-supervised one-on-one friendships with other well-behaved kids can be especially beneficial to a young child who is prone to aggression.

If, despite your efforts, the sparks do fly, then it's time for damage control. One mother of a habitual bully learned the best approach is to cooperate with everyone involved. She remembers being called into the school to find the administrators waiting for her, ready to pounce. "They hate you before you even get there," she says. But she found that if she didn't try to spread the blame onto them but rather presented herself as eager to help solve the problem, even going so far as to call the victim's mother and apologize for her son's action, she was able to let her son know that absolutely *no one* would tolerate that kind of behavior.

Such a unified approach requires commitment on the part of both parents and school. Unfortunately, that unity is not always there. As discussed earlier, a bully's parents are quite often bullies themselves. In that case, the school's commitment to wiping out bullying is critical. It may be a child's only hope.

HOW SCHOOLS CAN HELP

A school's approach to the problem can make or break a bully. There is a right way and a wrong way (more about this in Chapter 6).

The wrong approach may be the "soft" approach. Educators and child development experts have not had much success with private counselling, trying to teach troublesome youngsters that aggression is bad. Experts have tried therapy with aggressive children—helping them to avoid acting spontaneously, teaching them how to think and behave in a more controlled, peaceful way—but it rarely works when done in isolation, says Dr. David G. Perry, a professor at Florida Atlantic University who has researched childhood victimization. When the child returns to the classroom, all those wonderful lessons quickly disappear. It's tough to change your ways when everyone still thinks of you as a bully, expects you to act like a bully and you get such a satisfying rush of power when you do. It's such a buzz! Why stop?

That sensitive approach may work for other problems, but a more straight-forward approach seems to work best on bullies. A child who makes his way through life using the butt of his head will be much more influenced by direct non-hostile punishment, by discovering, in no uncertain terms, that bullying doesn't pay. In fact there are increasing calls for charges to be laid against bullies whenever possible. In Ontario, the provincial government has ordered its schools to report all acts of violence immediately to police. The order came after a 15-year-old girl was threatened with a knife on school property and school officials failed to notify either the girl's parents or the police.

Schools make the most headway with bullies when, like parents, they first set the ground rules—clear standards and expectations for behavior—and then follow through with lost privileges and time-out when the rules are broken.

Many teachers find that "good-behavior contracts" between the school, the bully and the bully's parents work well. Reaching out to the bully's parents can also help. Some schools have invited them to volunteer at recess or lunch to give them a stronger, more positive link with

MORE TIPS TO REDUCE AGGRESSION

- Rough play is normal among young children, but if you notice your child is deliberately hurting another, take a closer look at her behavior. It may be necessary to step in if things get too rowdy. Warn children that if they aren't careful, someone could actually get hurt. This reminds them that they really don't want to hurt anyone else, something that can easily get forgotten in the excitement.

- Nip bossiness in the bud and take the time to point out to pint-sized aggressors how their victim felt.

- Limit exposure to aggression on TV and in movies, violent games and toys. (See Chapter 7 for more on the effects of media violence.)

- Never tell a child that he must do something because you said so. That merely teaches him that might means right.

- Enforce good eating habits. Although the jury is still out on the link between diet and aggressive behavior, many teachers swear that kids are more aggressive after a morning breakfast of sugary cereal or after gorging on Easter or Hallowe'en treats. In fact there are some preliminary indications that there may be a relationship between food intolerance and criminal behavior. Your best bet is to make sure your child eats a balanced, healthy diet—especially at breakfast—so that, at the very least, he can better concentrate on his school work.

- Examine your own behavior and watch that you don't bully other people yourself. How do you handle the cashier who over-charges you, the spouse who burns dinner, the long line-up at the bank? Your children may model their behavior on yours. Let your child know it takes great strength not to fight, because it means you have some control over your emotions.

their child's school, and a better view of their child's behavior. Others have tried an in-school suspension in which the offender is forbidden to leave the "penalty box" (a room set aside for this purpose) for a set period of time. She is isolated from her friends, is accompanied to the washroom, eats her lunch in "the box" and is supervised to ensure she spends the time doing school work only. It's not nearly as appealing to offenders as the little holidays offered by the regular out-of-school suspensions.

Teachers face a difficult balancing act between compassion and discipline. There is often that niggling knowledge that the bully isn't all bad, that he has troubles of his own and needs help. There is also the very real possibility that the bully may be a victim also. In addition to punishment (which is still very important) teachers can provide rewarding opportunities for the bully to behave positively.

MAKING USE OF PEER PRESSURE

The bully is a natural leader. Taking away his opportunity for leadership is going to leave a void—and a very unhappy student. Bullying boils down to power. (It is no coincidence that in the 18th and 19th centuries, the word bully also meant "pimp.") The bully often wields power over his peers and, for an anti-bullying program to work, educators need to remember that the bully has become dependent on that power for his identity. So if you're going to take something away, you'd better replace it with something else.

Giving the bully an important role in the classroom—putting her in charge of the sports equipment, for example, or setting him up as a trained mediator of classroom disputes—gives him or her a chance to use these leadership talents in a positive way. A bully can develop empathy by helping another student who is having trouble with a subject, by assisting the teacher with preparations for the next day's class, or by designing anti-bully posters for the school.

Directing peer pressure can be another way to turn a negative into a positive. A school-wide campaign of compassion can work wonders. Children should be encouraged to look out for each other. Telling a teacher about a bully should not be negatively construed as being a tattletale and students should feel welcome to discuss behavior problems with teachers. A peer group that frowns on bullying can be a teacher's strongest ally.

Each classroom can make its own set of guidelines: a bully may forfeit time on the computers or clean black-boards at recess. The most powerful deterrent to a bully is being excluded from his peers. He'll learn that if he wants to play, he'll have to play nicely.

And finally, there is still room for the softer approach. Social-skills training programs and counselling that help bullies learn to ask, listen and communicate better can be beneficial when used in addition to clear consequences for bad behavior.

HOW THE COMMUNITY CAN HELP

A combined effort by the adult world can do a lot of good, but it is often stifled by a mind-your-own-business atti-tude. How other people raise their children is their own business, right?

One mother of a four-year-old child takes a different approach: "I know that some adults say, 'Oh well, kids will be kids.' But I don't believe that," she says. "As a responsible parent and a member of our society, if I see someone bullying another kid, I have to say something. This is our environment and community we're creating. If I saw someone rob a store, I'd phone the police."

Sometimes impartial observers, who may be neither parents nor teachers, have the clearest view of a bully's behavior. And sometimes those neutral community members can do a lot to help solve the problem:

- The community can lobby for better programs for at-risk moms and babies, aiming for healthy babies born to healthy, informed mothers, early home-visiting programs and high quality pre-school programs to stop bad habits before they are "hard-wired" into a child's brain.
- Extra-curricular groups like Scouts or Girl Guides can hold a wealth of positive social opportunities for the bully. Adult leaders who become aware of a bully in the community may be able to approach him or his parents tactfully and encourage him to join.
- Parenting-skills workshops can help guide the bully's parents.
- Crisis-intervention programs for battered women can help stop the cycle of violence with education and counselling programs for their children.
- Just being a good neighbor can help. Are there bullies roughing up a little one in the park next door? Shutting the blinds won't make the problem go away. If you can't stop the problem yourself—and with today's escalating conflicts, that may not be a good idea—then speak to the child's school or parents or police.

You don't wait for your house to be broken into before you start locking the doors at night. Similarly, as adults we should not wait for the loud little bully down the block to break the law before we start worrying about what went wrong. Bullying is everyone's problem. Solving the problem is everyone's responsibility.

4

Understanding the Victim

Fourteen-year-old Emma can't figure out what's wrong with her. Why do the other kids bully her all the time? A polite, soft-spoken girl, her childhood has been peppered with unkindness and she doesn't understand why.

In elementary school, girls she thought were her friends would suddenly turn on her, pushing her, calling her names, writing things about her on their binders and pencil cases. Their barbs cut to the bone. She hid her tears until she got home, then cried quietly in her bedroom at night. Now, in high school, another girl is tormenting her. Once she pushed Emma off her bicycle, shoving her head against the wall so roughly that she required stitches.

"Whenever someone bullied someone else, I'd always be there for them. No one but my mom was there for me. What hurts most is I was so nice back to them. Why did they have to be mean to me? I just don't understand."

What do you tell your child? What do you say when your heart is aching and your blood is boiling? This poor child has been selected, out of all the kids in his classroom or neighborhood, for persecution by his peers. Why?

Unfortunately, the answer isn't always clear.

It just seems to be the nature of the universe that some children go through life with a permanent "kick me" sign on their backs. As parents we may not know our child is an easy mark, but be assured the bullies do. And researchers aren't entirely certain why. It can be a simple matter of a shy child who is at the wrong place at the wrong time, or it can be more complex and chronic, a muddy, muddled mix of natural and environmental factors that have pushed our child down that rocky path alone.

THE FORGOTTEN VICTIM

The fact is, more is known about bullies than about their prey. Over the past few years there have been only a handful of studies carried out on victims. While there is a plenitude of psychologists and child development experts who specialize in aggression, only a few look at the victims, mainly because the bully's behavior problem is much more salient. His behavior makes you angry, it disrupts the classroom, it's tough to ignore.

And it's not easy for researchers to classify victims: some are bullied only briefly—for a few days, weeks or months—and others find their torment dragged out over an extended period of time. For some, like Emma, the bullying can last years.

So while parents, police and educators scramble to clean up the bully's messes and child development experts struggle to find out what went wrong, the youngsters at the receiving end—who seem to be quiet and relatively well-behaved children—are easily forgotten. To the adult world they are often unknown, misunderstood or sometimes conveniently classified as unlikeable and dismissed.

Quite often when an adult is confronted with the problem, he or she will assume the victim has done something to deserve his trouble. One girl who was regularly victimized kept her mouth shut for just that reason. She says she was afraid to say anything to her teacher because she figured she'd be ignored or trivialized. The teacher had once told her parents that she was "an unlikeable kid." That just confirmed in her mind that she couldn't count on adults coming to her aid. A teenager now, it still hurts her to think of it.

By shunting the victim aside, adults are reinforcing one of the characteristics that make him vulnerable in the first place: isolation. A victim is a victim because he is alone.

Whatever else they might be, bullies aren't stupid. They don't direct their anger in a haphazard way. They choose targets who are appropriate. That usually means children who are not only alone but who look like loners. They have that lost look, a kind of body language that kids read well. They are the ones who won't talk back, hit back or come back for retaliation.

A bully remembers the way he and a friend tormented a shy little boy when the teacher was out of the room: "The first time we did this, we fully expected to get punished when Miss Bradshaw realized what had transpired. However, Gary didn't tell her, nor did anyone else. I realized that Gary was not a member of any clique. He would never put up a challenge." The knowledge was exhilarating! The two bullies knew they now had free reign to do just about anything.

Studies show habitual victims are unlikely to have reliable friends. The few friends they have are also on the fringe. Bullies know this kid is safe to pick on because she'll take it alone. Her friends are not the type to step in and help out. In the childhood hierarchy, she's stuck at the bottom.

PHYSICAL CHARACTERISTICS OF THE VICTIM

Being a loner does not necessarily mean a child is going to be bullied. There are other factors. A major one is body size. You've got good protection against being bullied if you're big and strong. But if you're small or weak, watch out. In the boyhood race for popularity, weakness and strength are crucial factors, even among teenagers. The old muscle-building ad in the back of the comic book was pretty accurate after all.

Various researchers have discovered that many other physical differences can single out a child as a potential victim. It doesn't take much; it's just an excuse for the bullies, a reason to tease somebody—anybody. Bullies and their classmates are the judge and jury; the child's crime is looking or acting differently. And the list of possible "crimes" is long: she may be younger, fatter, skinnier or smaller than the rest of the class; he may wear glasses, have physical handicaps, hearing problems, or speech or language difficulties. She may have an unusual appearance or a skin color that differs from the majority of the class, or a different facial expression, posture or dress. He may be super-eager to please, have supposedly irritating mannerisms or be considered a bit of a klutz.

Children with learning disabilities or behavioral problems are frequently targeted for harassment. One survey found that 38 per cent of special education students, compared to 18 per cent of other students, reported being bullied more than once or twice.[1] The learning-disabled child often plays with children who are younger than she, and then finds herself dislocated from her peer group, misunderstood, sometimes hyperactive, with mannerisms that rub others the wrong way.

Patricia, mother of a seven-year-old learning-disabled boy who suffers at school, can attest to that. Her son is teased constantly. It surprises her and, of course, angers her. She thought that with integrated classrooms youngsters today were more tolerant. Not so. Patricia and her son have learned that childhood is a competitive place that doesn't always compensate for differences or disabilities.

THE VICTIM'S PERSONALITY

And yet solitude or physical differences alone won't always lead to bullying. Often several other personality traits combine to wave the red flag, attracting the bully's attention and making the child vulnerable to long-term harassment. Usually these are the characteristics that aren't considered attractive or desirable in today's society. Victims are often misfits in a cutthroat climate; their big "mistake" is in simply being a little hesitant and insecure, a little too placid.

Dr. Dan Olweus has gathered a clear, depressing personality profile of the child who is a habitual victim. According to Olweus, the victim is likely to:

- be introverted and anxious, cautious, sensitive and quiet;

- commonly react to the bully's attacks with tears (at least in lower grades) and withdrawal;
- choose to nurse his wounds in private, rather than make a fuss;
- feel stupid, ashamed and unattractive;
- see himself as a failure.

Habitual victims often don't retaliate because they figure they're not worth it; their self-esteem is so poor that they justify the bully's attacks in their own minds and come to believe they deserve the persecution.

Other studies show they frequently feel depressed and rejected by their peers. The typical victim probably has a best friend, but that friendship is often a little off-kilter in the same way his relationship with his parents is off-kilter. His friendship is not a positive one. He often feels alienated, and communication with that friend (who is also probably on the social fringes) tends to be weak. Victims may easily become afraid or cry and, if they're male, avoid taking part in rough games. They feel alone, lonely and disliked.

Remember that irritating little kid in elementary school who just sort of bugged everybody and you never really knew why? The class dork or pest or jerk (labels as stark and jarring as a slap in the face), the kid who never really fit in? Psychologists think they know why he didn't fit. They have found that these children may have subtle deficiencies in the way they send and receive non-verbal messages. For some reason, these youngsters are unable to recognize unspoken signals or communicate their emotions without words. Facial expressions, posture, gestures, interpersonal distance, tone of voice or cloth-ing—they manage to get it all wrong. They may stand too closely, touch inappropriately or misinterpret others' non-verbal communications.[2]

These are kids who seem to lack the ingredient that makes others street-smart or people-savvy. Immigrant children may be at particular risk if they arrive in an area in which their own race doesn't predominate, since they can have trouble reading unspoken messages delivered in an unfamiliar cultural context. Their slightly "off" behavior makes them stand out and bugs their classmates, though neither the newcomers nor the more established children really know why. They are prime targets for bullying.

HOW SHYNESS CAN LEAD TO VICTIMIZATION

Sometimes a child can send out signals at an early age that he is victim-prone and in for a hard time. They are signals that parents are first to pick up on. Some moms and dads of victims say their children showed signs of being cautious and sensitive at a very young age. Studies have found that anxious school-aged children were unadaptable and easily distressed as infants and toddlers.

CHARACTERISTICS OF THE TYPICAL VICTIM

He or she
- is a loner or has few friends on the fringe;
- is weak or small or has some physical difference, anything from buck teeth to a weird haircut;
- is quiet, anxious, unassertive, eager to please and quick to concede;
- socially immature;
- may have a physical or learning disability;
- may have an over-protective mother, critical, uninvolved father or a domineering sibling.

It may be something they were born with. There is evidence that the behavior of a typically shy child—gaze-aversion and withdrawal in conflict, the sort of demeanor that invites bullying—may be inherent and even inherited. Studies show that the majority of children who seemed shy as toddlers were still shy in elementary school. But there's evidence these placid, cautious, sensitive children would have done just fine if it weren't for their being bullied. Once the bully's ball starts rolling, it's hard to stop it. And if it isn't stopped quickly, the child can become all tangled up in a cycle of victimization.

In the beginning, when they first start school, they may be the quiet ones in class. On the playground, they may watch from afar. They may want to join in with the others, but aren't as socially skilled, are afraid or are deferential around other kids. And at first their behavior isn't noticed by the other kids, except perhaps to earn them the label of shy.

They are the kind of children parents and teachers love, the little angels. Obedient, compliant, constructive, they try hard to please and the teachers reinforce their behavior because it's so much easier to deal with. They can leave them in their quiet little corner and concentrate on those irritating squeaky wheels.

But those same pleasant personality traits lead them to be vulnerable and easily influenced. And they may lead them right into the clutches of the schoolyard bully, because as children reach the ages of seven to nine and become more socially competent, mature and outgoing, the shy little one's sedentary and passive behavior begins to stand out.

Until the age of seven, a bully will target everyone and anyone, shopping, in a sense, for just the right victim. As

THE VICTIM CYCLE

kids make the move to new peer groups (new classes, new schools), bullies may "sample" other children's responses by acting aggressively towards them. Those who submit to the aggression, cry, appear anxious or upset or give up their possessions, reveal themselves as easy marks. And from then on, the bully focuses his attention on them. That may be why at the beginning of the year about 22 per cent of children report having been victimized, but by the end of the year only 8 per cent say they are regularly bullied.[3]

It may be during these years that his self-esteem takes the biggest battering. His naturally quiet, docile temperament leads him right into trouble: somebody taunts him, maybe playfully at first or engages him in some light rough-housing. His passive, sensitive response leads to more intense teasing. Name-calling begins, which isolates and dehumanizes him in the eyes of other classmates. His self-esteem plummets. He shows more sensitivity and passivity. He is bullied more often, in more public venues, in an increasingly systematic and hurtful way. His self-esteem falls further, and so on.... He is caught in the bully's web of pain.

But again, that shyness on its own doesn't mean those children are destined to be bullied. Usually it takes some sort of environmental exacerbation, according to Lynne Henderson, director of the Palo Alto Shyness Clinic in California: "Victimhood is how you look at the world, whether you're able and willing to reach out for help."

The consistent victim is beyond shy. There are different kinds of shyness. One is fear of novelty, which most of us experience to varying degrees. Then there is a wariness of evaluation by others. In some kids, this wariness drives them away from others. They don't know how to initiate and sustain interaction with other kids; they are either abrasive or they hover. Assimilating into a group is tough. These kids are most at risk for victimization.

And they're especially at risk if they are male. Boys who are shy, sedentary and sensitive unfortunately don't fit in with our rock-'em sock-'em stereotype of what a boy ought to be. For this reason they are often rejected by classmates and grownups alike. In fact some early studies show that teachers don't really accept those unstereotypical little boys, and being rejected by the adult world only reinforces the child's isolation.

THE CHRONIC VICTIM: A HINT OF TROUBLE AHEAD?

There are degrees of victimization. Some children who are a little shy or hesitant or different-looking may be bullied briefly—for a few weeks or months or even several terms at school. It's a painful experience, and it may affect their outlook on life and their self-image, but it is not a reflection of a deviant personality. They've just had the misfortune of being at the wrong place, among the wrong people, at the wrong time.

For some others, however, it's a different story. The

victim role is just something they can't seem to shake. Whatever the setting, whatever the milieu, these kids have a really hard go of it. They may transfer schools only to have the victim role follow them there. Or they may find themselves bullied for years. Or they may find themselves in the role of victim, then bully, then victim, never really fitting in, their social life fraught with pain and conflict. They are often socially immature and provocative—they may interrupt other children's activity, avoid eye contact, make provocative remarks. They probably have few friends and are not very well liked. The chronic victim sometimes adopts a "victim mentality." He comes to believe that he deserves the bullying, and even looks for it, seeking attention of any kind. He may often put himself down, reject compliments, feel convinced no one likes him and that he can do no good. Rejected by his peers, he has little opportunity to learn friendship skills and so the chasm widens.

For these children, being bullied may be a sign of deeper troubles—psychosocial troubles that could lead to difficulties for them later in life.

One of the clearest indications of that comes from studies that followed girls who were chronic victims or both bullies and victims into their teenage years. These girls are shown to have higher levels of sexually transmitted disease, gynecological problems, pregnancy and childbirth during their teen years.

Even more disturbing: the children these troubled and troublesome girls give birth to may also be headed for trouble. Studies show that mothers who were bullies when young may be more neglecting, inconsistent and unresponsive towards their offspring, who in turn suffer more developmental delays. And mothers who were chronic victims suffer from depression more often and may be less likely to provide their children with stimulating play materials.[4]

Researcher Lisa Serbin says she is horrified at the amount of hospitalization suffered by children of chronic victims. Studies show these kids have triple the number of emergency hospitalizations related to injury. It is not clear whether the injuries were a result of accident or abuse. Nor is it known whether the victimization causes the mother to be a poor parent. What is more likely, Serbin and others say, is that these children were chosen by their peers to be bullied because of their inadequate social behavior—behavior which also may lead them to make other mistakes. Being bullied probably only exacerbated their problems.

What this tells us is that children with these more severe social difficulties need special help. The child who is constantly victimized is the child we should be especially concerned about. She may be in need of guidance and support, therapy and training to help her deal with rejection, depression and social interaction before she passes on her psychosocial problems to the next generation.

*   *   *

When you have been judged by a jury of your peers and come up short for extremely nebulous reasons, when your so-called crime, be it shyness or attitude or physical difference, is so shrouded in secret, subtle shadows that even the bully doesn't quite understand what bugs him about you, it can be very, very hard to take.

It may be even harder to take than when the reasons are more obvious, as they are in racist-inspired bullying. Kevin, who remembers being bullied because he was of an ethnic background that differed from the rest of his neighborhood, figures it was a little easier for him to shrug off the effects because, he says, he can understand what's behind it. It may be better to stick out like a sore thumb than to irritate like a nagging, invisible little hangnail.

THE VICTIM'S FAMILY LIFE

Smart little Tim used to live in fear of big Gord and his cronies. Gord had been failed at school once or twice and his recess-time hobby was tormenting Tim. Today, Tim has grown up and is raising two children, but he still doesn't understand. "What did I do to deserve it? I was just a normal kid who minded his own business, rather cheerful, polite and conscientious."

But his father was just the opposite. "He was the controlling type who created an elaborate mythology to keep his children at bay." Dad bragged of his fighting ability, embellishing stories when needed. During arguments he'd challenge his son to come outside and settle it with his fists. "I bought into it and the arguments ended when I didn't want to get into a physical fight with him." Tim now thinks his father's bullying him led him to be a "pleaser" and the class victim.

Tim is probably right. Much of what goes on in the playground simply reflects what goes on in the home. Family relationships—especially with moms and dads—that aren't entirely healthy can lead a child to be a bully or a victim. It is common knowledge among educators and those who work with children that withdrawal or bullying sometimes is a signal that there may be violence or abuse in the child's home.

However, the abuse can often be extremely subtle. Sometimes it's not abuse at all but simply ineffective parenting. During the early years, how well a family monitors its children and teaches good problem-solving skills influences whether a child will be victimized. As children grow older, however, how the family deals with their kids' independence becomes much more important. In some families, when a child reaches adolescence, a rift develops. The child may feel very attached to, and at the same time alienated from, a parent because that parent has not given him the normal amount of independence and decision-making power of adolescence. These kids are more likely to become victims. Studies show victims' mothers tended to be overanxious and over-protective. (Over-protection is defined by the degree to which the mother treats the boy as younger than his age, and how controlling and restrictive she is regarding his activities with friends and during his spare time.)

Thus a mother who tended to treat her son as younger than his age, prevented him from independent behavior and was highly controlling may have increased his chance of being bullied. However, a boy who is quiet and placid may elicit extra attention and protection from his mom. Her overinvolvement may simply be a normal response to her child's temperament.

The victim's father may be the opposite: critical, withdrawn and distant. In his studies Dr. Olweus says the boy victim seldom wanted to be like his father, while dad thought of his son as not very "boyish." It may be that this poor relationship, coupled with the boy's inability to identify with males, causes the unassertive, seemingly unmasculine behavior that grabs a bully's attention.

Although parental factors are less important among victims than among bullies, there are surprising similarities between bullies and victims. Researchers have found both types may come from hostile homes where discipline is harsh and inconsistent. The chronic victim's problems may have the same roots as the career bully. Some experts feel that both behavior types are linked to an insecure attachment to the child's parents during the first few years of life. It does seem to be a factor in the most severe cases of victimization: the kids who get trapped in their roles as victims and who take years to extricate themselves.

Why these insecure attachments arise is still uncertain. Some researchers believe that every child arrives in the world with certain characteristics that can be exacerbated or inhibited, depending on the parents' reaction. If a baby appears to be shy, for example, his or her parents will treat their child in a different manner from, say, an outgoing, vocal baby.

This insecurity can also stem from a parent who is either insensitive or unresponsive to the child's need. When a parent responds appropriately to a child's call for help, the child develops a belief that she can have an effect on her world. But an unhealthy relationship can develop if the child cries and the caregiver consistently does not respond. Or if the child tries to accomplish something on his own and the caregiver leaps right in and does it for him. Either way, the child feels thwarted and frustrated.

Gradually he develops a lack of trust, an image that this is a parent whom he cannot count on for support. And then, from the age of 13 months on, this feeling expands into the growing belief that this is a world he can't count on for support.

When an insecure attachment develops, some children respond in a hostile way (like the bully) while others withdraw from the world. It can be seen in the different ways a 12-month-old may respond to a completely new setting. The typical response in a child of that age is to stay by mom in the beginning but eventually to move away, occasionally smiling and glancing back at her as the reference point. Slowly the child risks moving farther and farther away from his mother, the need to explore outweighing the slight worry, and in the end he settles down, knowing he can always come back to her.

But trouble may be down the road for the toddler who simply plops himself down with some toys and doesn't bother to look back at mom or chase after her should she leave his sight. These kids may have had neglecting, unresponsive caregivers when they were babies and are attempting to deal with angry, hostile feelings. Children who respond in this way tend to become biters and hitters when they get a little older.

There may be trouble in the works, too, for the child who reacts in the opposite way to the novel situation, who refuses to leave his mom's side, becomes extremely distraught when she tries to leave and has no impulse whatsoever to explore the room. Sometimes this is the future victim, a baby who has been over-protected or "smothered."

Finally, a child's relationships with brothers and sisters can have an effect on who is bullied and who is not. In the best possible world, siblings are teachers of life. From their brothers or sisters, children learn social skills, assertiveness and how to curb aggression. Unfortunately, things don't always work out that way. And when they don't, problems erupt outside the home too.

> *"My big brother bullies me," ten-year-old Justine confesses. "The way he does things really bothers me. When he doesn't get his way he hits me or says mean things. Being bothered by my brother makes me really angry and I want to hurt him. Since I'm smaller than him I can't hit him. He'll just hurt me more. When he's in a bad mood I stay out of his way."*
>
> *Justine's friend confirms this account. "Every recess he comes up to her and kicks her, punches her, trips her and pulls her hair. So every time the bell rings at the end of recess, she comes to the line crying and tells us the same thing: 'My brother beat me up.' She says it makes her feel like she wants to go over there and kill him."*

Pain like that is not easily erased. The victim of a bully harbors a deep, secret pain that festers in silence; it may never be forgotten or forgiven.

Bullying among siblings is especially potent because of its permanent nature. Justine's brother is her brother forever. He will always be older than she is; he will probably always be bigger. And not only is he causing her great pain and fear now, but his bullying is setting a pattern for future relationships. He has discovered a tremendous rush of power when he dominates someone else. And she has learned how to be a victim.

Chances are good, though, that both sister and brother, for a variety of reasons, are keeping their mouths shut.

Mom and dad may not have a clue. And this is one of the scariest aspects of the bully problem.

WHY THE VICTIM DOESN'T SEEK HELP

"I was nine years old. He was the most popular boy and all of the girls liked him. But I was always aware that, to him, I didn't rate." The bully's teasing escalated to punching and kicking. After every school day Sarah raced out the door, but he and his buddies inevitably caught her, knocked her to the ground and banged her head on the hard, gravelly snow.

She screamed for help. Her classmates watched but did nothing.

She lied to her parents about her cuts and bruises. Eventually, though, her parents caught on. Ashamed, Sarah denied it. Her father had to resort to following her to school, trying to find out who was doing the bullying. Her parents then secretly searched through the class photographs like mug shots until they identified the culprit. Finally, faced with such overwhelming evidence, she admitted to her parents she had a problem.

Calm, rational adults that we are, it's hard to understand. How could such unkindness be kept secret? Why did no one speak up to the adult world? Most of all, why did Sarah try to hide her pain and protect the bully?

In fact this conspiracy of silence is quite common. To youngsters the idea of tattling is terrifying. It's all wrapped up in their minds with helplessness, isolation and violating loyalty. Unwittingly they ascribe to a covert classroom conspiracy, similar to the one that keeps child abuse hidden: tell, and you're dead.

So parents and teachers may go merrily along without detecting a hint of trouble. Researchers say parents of both victims and bullies are generally unaware of bullying problems at school and rarely discuss the issue with their children.[5] The shootings in Littleton, Colorado, and Tabor, Alberta, threw a spotlight on bullying, however, and it is hoped that today's parents may be discussing the issue more—a welcome change considering students say bullying happens much more frequently than their parents believe. In one study,[6] 49 per cent of the children said they'd been bullied at least once or twice during the term. But only 32 per cent of parents believed bullying had taken place.

Sadly, it's often the most badly victimized who report it least. Interviews reveal children are afraid that adults will underreact or overreact and make the problem worse. And adults are busy with more important matters; why trouble them over *their* minor problems? Or they are afraid of the bully coming back at them. Often they are ashamed because they can't stand up for themselves, or because they feel they share some of the guilt for being the object of bullying. Or they believe adults are simply not up to the job of protecting them.

"You've got to be seen as cool," explains a 15-year-old girl from a small town. "No one wants to be a tattletale. And besides, the bullies are really threatening. They'll get you back if you tell."

Throughout a child's growing-up years he unquestioningly follows a hidden code of behavior imposed and enforced by his classmates. From the minute he enters interactive relationships with other children, he is bombarded with childhood's rules of conduct. They are rules that give life to those judgmental insults like "snitch," "sissy," "squealer," "tattletale." Remember the most cutting one of all? "O-o-oh, so you have to run to your *mommy*!" Those wisecracks were keeping mouths shut when we were young and they are still around today, doing their muzzling dirty work.

That feeling of helplessness and isolation extends into the high-school years and contributes to the problem of gang retribution and group bullying. As one teenager said, "The teachers don't do nothing. All we got is ourselves. If you get jumped, if some guy jumps you, you get them back. You don't care if it doesn't solve anything. It's just payback."

What's the point in telling adults? young people want to know. Grownups won't or can't do anything about it anyway. It doesn't help when the media is presenting the worst cases as everyday occurrences, when newspapers and news shows regularly broadcast violence and unchecked youth melees. It helps create a kind of cynicism towards the adult world that is demonstrably failing to protect them. It gives them a panicky, paranoid feeling of abandonment.

A 14-year-old boy was approached in the park and followed home by a man demanding sex. When he got home, he told his mother, who called the police. The police did nothing. Not long after that incident, the boy was swarmed by a group of bullies and his Chicago Bulls cap was stolen. This time, he didn't report it. Why should he? Obviously his experiences aren't important enough to rate any attention.

WARNING SIGNS: IS YOUR CHILD BEING BULLIED?
- unexplained bruises, scrapes, torn clothing;
- nightmares;
- headaches, stomach aches;
- overtired, not sleeping or not eating;
- evasiveness, sullenness;
- out-of-character behavior;
- temper outbursts; bullies siblings
- increased absences from school;
- more time spent in his or her bedroom;
- doesn't want to go to school, or take the bus;
- frequently loses toys, clothing (many kids today say they lost their jacket on the bus or subway when it has really been stolen by bullies);
- is ravenous when he or she returns home from school (lunch money or lunch pail may be getting stolen);
- fears school, wants a ride there and back and wants you to pick him or her up as soon as the bell rings.

These signs, on their own, do not necessarily mean your child is being bullied, but they should make you suspicious. Remember that some children have been known to commit suicide over bullying. Don't take such threats lightly—seek professional help.

Ever since Matt was a toddler, his mom asked him about his day as she tucked him in at night. "Who did you play with?" Kate would ask. "What did you do at recess?" Lately, though, Matt's responses were brief. "Nobody." "No one." With a bit of probing, Kate found out that the boys were not letting Matt play soccer at recess. She bought him a soccer ball and told him to start his own game. A few weeks later, she followed up. No one wanted to play with Matt's ball. James, one of the boys in his grade, had somehow crowned himself king of the playground and all the boys chose to play with him. What's more, the pint-sized king had decided Matt could not join in. "Do you want me to talk to the school about it?" Kate asked. Matt was adamant. No way. Kate suggested he find some other kids to play with and let it pass. A few weeks later, when it appeared Matt was still being excluded, Kate decided to check it out. She slipped out of work during her lunch hour and drove to the school parking lot. Watching from her car window she could see Matt behind the soccer goal line pretending to be the goalie, though the real goalie was directly in front of him. At one point the ball came to Matt and, lost in the excitement, he caught it and threw it back into the game. Enraged, one of the players took off after him, threw him to the ground and began kicking him. Kate had one foot out the door, uncertain whether or not to embarrass her son further by coming to his rescue, when the soccer players called the other boy back into the game. Matt picked himself up and walked right back to the goal line again. Hunched down in the car, Kate felt sick that she had let it go on for so long. That day she spoke to the teacher. Thanks to a swift, sensitive response from the school, the playground king now knows why he should not exclude others from the game, the other players have learned that exclusion is unacceptable, and Matt is finally, fully immersed in play at recess, having learned the lesson that adults can help after all.

As adults, parents, teachers, caregivers and community leaders, we have a job to do. We must wipe out that feeling of helplessness. Children are not helpless; the bully is not omnipotent. We are here to help them. But we must be committed to help and our children must know it. The following chapters examine the important role grownups have in battling the schoolyard bully.

5

Helping the Victim:
The Parents' Role

*Tom was a quiet boy who didn't do well in sports
and suffered from poor self-esteem. He accepted
teasing and name-calling as his lot in life. His
buddy David had the same problem. One day
after school a few of the tough guys stopped
them on the way home from school, threatening
to beat them up. Tom ran away in fear. David
stayed behind to defend himself. Tom was
unscathed, but terrified of the next encounter.
David was badly beaten. The next day David's
father came to school to discuss the problem
with school authorities. He let the school know
in no uncertain terms that bullying was not
acceptable and that he hoped the teachers
would do something to eradicate it. He also
pointed out to Tom that, in running away, he
hadn't been a very good friend to David. "Even
today," says Tom, now a small-town minister, "I*

*remember the incident with shame because I ran
away in fear and because I left my friend
behind."*

In a typical bullying incident, there are two automatic
responses: fight or flight. Tom took one, his friend took
the other. Neither response, however, worked particularly well. And if David's dad hadn't stepped in, the
bullies might have carried on their bullying indefi-
nitely. It finally took an adult to put a stop to it. It
usually does.

Adults may like to think bullying is a child's business,
but it's not. It's grownups' business too. As a parent, you
have a big role to play. Your approach to the problem
determines your child's approach to the problem. And
that approach can make or break the victim-bully cycle.
What do you do: ignore it? Storm over to the school or to
the bully's parents? Tell your child to fight or flee or bow
down and take it?

None of that, really. It's much more complicated. You
don't want to solve the problem for her, nor do you want
to abandon her in her time of need. You want to guide her
gently through her bout with the bully and, to do so, there
are three important steps:

1. Help the child figure out what to do on an immediate basis, when face-to-face with the bully.
2. Follow through on an adult level after the incident
   to ensure the child is protected and the bully is
   punished.
3. Prepare the child for the next encounter and,
   ideally, help her avoid it altogether.

FACE-TO-FACE: FIGHT OR FLIGHT?

Most children believe the only way to cope with bullies is to avoid them and to stay with friends. But to a shy child who doesn't have many friends, that may not be possible. When face-to-face with a bully, the victim is on his own and he knows it. The problem may seem insurmountable and overwhelming, especially when, if he does gather up the courage to ask for adult help, all he gets back are the pat old axioms that are either outdated, confusing or misleading.

- A father who hopes to raise a peace-loving human being tells his child to "turn the other cheek." The child does and gets his other cheek whopped.
- Another parent tells her child to run away. The bully runs faster.
- "Punch him back, as hard as you can," mom tells her daughter. The bully punches harder.

These kids can tell you that the pat little formulas just don't work. In any bullying episode, the mix of power plays and peer pressure is just too complex for such snug, smug, simple stuff. And giving a child rigid, formulaic advice—in Situation A, use Tactic #3—will leave a child in a quandary if it fails. Adults can do more by helping the child create her own solutions that don't include more violence, hitting back or "giving the bully a taste of his own medicine."

WHY YOUR CHILD SHOULD NOT HIT BACK

Four young girls were swimming in the local pool one day when another group of girls began tossing insults their way. "We'll get you later," the bullies warned the group of four girls. Sure enough, they did.

"We soon spotted them hiding behind some trees, waiting for us," Clare remembers. "With eyes as big as saucers, pounding hearts and rapidly moving little legs, we tried to make a run for it."

One of the biggest girls caught Clare's friend. "Without thinking I marched up to the brute who was holding my friend and punched her right in the stomach, grabbed my friend's hand and we ran all the way home. I faced my fear that day and was richer for it. I believe that bullies are a necessary evil in life. Confronting bullies is a necessary skill, especially today. Facing fear is really what it's all about."

It's surprising how nostalgia can make violence look courageous, noble and triumphant. Surprising how time can dull fear, soften brutality and make it seem all rosy and right. Many adults carry in their knapsack of memories fond recollections of how they decked the school bully. They are the ones for whom the fight-back strategy worked.

It's hard to argue with success. That's what has led to the platitudes being handed down through generations: "Don't start a fight but make sure you finish it." Or, "Be sure to make that first blow count." And it's led some parents to give shockingly violent advice.

They were a group of friends who had known each other since way back when. Now, with kids of their own, they loved to get together to talk about old times. Unfortunately, there was one

*child in their group whom nobody could stand—
a real bully. Once, when he was picking on
Jennifer, her mom got fed up. "Stay still for a
minute, Jonathan," she ordered the little bully.
"Okay Jennifer," she told her daughter, "hit him
as hard as you can." Jonathan's mom, who was
standing right there, was completely aghast. But
Jennifer's mom was satisfied. Jonathan the bully
never bothered Jennifer the hitter again.*

Sure it worked. So does child abuse. So does battering a
spouse. No question, aggression can be very successful.
But is it right?

Dr. Debra Pepler, a psychology professor at York
University, who has spent the last 15 years studying
aggression in youngsters, recalls the time she was giving
a talk on the subject to a group of parents. The principal
of the school was anxious to have her speak because, the
previous week, one of his students had been seriously
injured by a bully and the parents were extremely
concerned. After Pepler gave her speech, one of the mothers stood up. "What you said is fine," she said, "but I just
tell my kid to hit back. What's wrong with that?" Hitting
back is an issue that never fails to be raised during a
discussion about bullying, Pepler says.

Pepler explained to this particular parent why that
approach is wrong. "I can't argue that it's not effective in
some situations. It may well be," she told her. "But on
many occasions the problems simply accelerate and the
child is at an increased risk. It's not a positive way to
solve the problem and it teaches kids yet again to use
aggression. And finally, it's not calling on the adult
resources in the community that should be dealing with

this kind of thing. If there is an adult environment in which all a child has to do is talk to an adult and there's swift action, and if the child knows that, and if he has other negotiating strategies to help him deal with bullying, then he won't have to resort to hitting back."

Afterwards, the principal told Pepler he was dumbfounded. The mother who had stood up and asked this question was the mother of the child who had been hospitalized after the bully's attack. It appears that the child was being bullied before and did what her mother had suggested: cuffed the bully back. The bully simply pulled the child off the playground and attacked her with a weapon. But this parent still had no recognition that her advice may have caused the problem to heat up so seriously.

Despite Canada's peacemaking reputation, Canadian children seem to be surprisingly aggressive. When presented with the "fight or flight" choice, Canadian kids often choose to fight. A study by Health and Welfare Canada found Canadian children were more likely to be confrontational with a bully than those in Belgium, Austria, Scotland or Hungary. While children in these other countries said they would rather do nothing or try to get away from a bully, the majority of Canadian young people who were surveyed said they would rather shout back at their harassers than retreat.[1]

When struggling over whether or not to hit back, a child should ask himself if hitting back will make the problem smaller. It's a good bet it won't. It is a myth that the bully will retreat if the victim fights back. That's why he usually picks weaker victims; he knows, if push comes to shove, he'll get the last shove. In fact most experts say that if the child hits back, he just tends to make the bully angrier. When two siblings fight and the younger child hits back, the older one never says, "Geez, I better leave him alone." The bully may be tough, but he's not stupid.

Besides, it won't work with a small, timid child. It's just not in her nature. As ten-year-old Angela describes it: "I'm always hurt by bullies. They call me names like 'fatso' and 'tub,' but I just try to ignore them. Having your feelings hurt by a bully makes you feel mad and hurt inside. Some people who have enough courage would probably want to make fun of them back." But for quiet little Angela, retaliation is out of the question.

Even bullies will agree that hitting back may not be wise. Angela's tormentor has this to offer: "Some people think I'm a bully. Maybe I am. I admit sometimes I'm mean," he shrugs. "I think if you get bullied you should tell a teacher. Don't fight back. You'll just get in more trouble if you fight back."

TIPS FOR VICTIMS
Here are some suggestions you can pass on to your children.
- If you're face-to-face with a bully, breathe deeply and imagine that you're wearing a special bully-proof overcoat to make the bully's barbs bounce off you. It won't be so fun for the bully if you pretend he's not bothering you.
- Give him a stone-faced stare — look right through the bully. Or try saying something totally unexpected. If the bully says, "You've got a funny nose," say, "I know I do." It may just take the wind out of the bully's sails.
- Try talking to the bully. Say calmly, forcefully, "I don't like it when…. Please stop" or "Why are you doing that?" or "Why are you angry at me?" Practice "standing tall" in front of the mirror or with your parents so that you can capture that assertive tone. You want to let him know that you are not afraid and that you will not stand for it.

Then take these steps to make sure it doesn't happen again:
- Be friendly with everyone.
- If you're shy, don't let it get you down. Lots of people feel shy, even adults. Just keep trying, help others if they seem shy, ask questions about other people and try to stop being so self-conscious.
- Stay with a group, don't be last in the change room, school hallway or washroom.
- Leave your valuable possessions at home.
- If you are being excluded from a group, try phoning a weaker member of the group, or one who used to be a close friend. Ask her why she is doing this, and assure her that you know she is a nice person and would never really want to hurt someone. Ask her for ideas to solve the problem, or suggest you meet with her and a few other "gentler" kids in the group to discuss what's happening.

STEP-BY-STEP THROUGH A FACE-TO-FACE

Responding with your brain, not your fists, can be a much more effective approach to an ugly encounter. (And this, of course, is a life-long rule.) Parents can help by teaching children to follow these steps to guide them through a face-to-face encounter.

Suggest your child do the following:

1. Try to ignore the bully.
2. If that doesn't work, talk to him in a friendly manner: ask questions, repeat back what you hear, make a funny, inoffensive comeback. (This takes practice; see section on role-playing later in this chapter.)
3. Failing that, calmly walk away. Remember to hide your fear.
4. If he follows, tell him you do not like what he is doing and will not put up with it. Keep walking and repeat yourself until you have walked to an adult who can help.
5. If these steps don't work and the bullying keeps up, then it's time to tell an adult. Warn the bully that this will be your next step if he doesn't stop. He may say "Make me,"

or call you a wuss or tattletale. Ignore that, and remember you are showing courage by standing up for yourself. If, when you do report to the adult, it is not taken seriously enough, report it again. Make sure, though, that the adult promises to keep your identity a secret.

This last step—telling an adult—is a huge one for children.

THE TATTLETALE TABOO

Emma had a boyfriend when she was in Grade 7. Six months later they broke up. Then, in Grade 9, his big sister Betty began to bully her. Betty called her names and she and her friends threw food at Emma in the cafeteria. Through it all she kept quiet. No way would she ever tattle. One day Betty pushed her off her bike and Emma's face was badly cut. She could hide the bullying no longer. She "confessed" to her father. She says that admitting her victimization hurt more than the bully's blows.

The stigma against tattling is pervasive and deep-rooted. It is a taboo that is reinforced in the adult world. Nobody likes a tattletale. Even teachers hate to encourage tattling, cringing at the thought of all those earnest little faces lining up at their desks ready to tell on so-and-so for doing such-and-such, seeking brownie points and the teacher's attention.

And yet it is not a long stretch of the imagination to extend a link from the schoolyard code of silence to the mafia's powerful muzzling of witnesses who wish to testify in court. Tattling is really just good citizenship. Adults, and society in general, need to change their attitude towards tattling before children can change theirs.

In a 1989 survey of bullying in ten Scottish secondary schools, half of the children who had been bullied had told no-one. Of the victims who had told, 47 per cent had told a parent and 31 per cent a teacher.[2] In a child's mind, snitching on the bully implies weakness and failure. It can make her feel like a traitor to her fellow students. It can signify to him that he is giving up, and his hope of making friends and joining in with the crowd is forever dashed. She may feel she is reinforcing her role as outcast by crossing over to the grownups' side. But the biggest obstacle of all may be fear. What if the bully finds out and comes back, angrier than ever? Who will protect her then? Fear of retaliation is the most effective muzzle of all.

> *"There's this one guy in my class who makes fun of people, of last names or how we look," says Carly, who attends Grade 6 in a small rural school. "It makes me feel dumb or funny-looking. I don't really know how to cope or get bullies off my back. I ignore them, but that only helps a bit. It would be good to tell the teacher but they could just beat you up even more. I don't know what to do."*

Children need to be impressed with the importance of telling an adult, with the guarantee that their identity will be protected if they do. And they need to know the difference between a "tattletale"—someone who is telling on kids because they're looking for attention—and legitimate tattling—reporting something that will help another person or that they have not been able to deal with on their own. For both young children and older ones, tattling is essential, for different reasons. At the primary-school age, children have few strategies to deal with bullying on their own and an adult's intervention is usually the only way out. At an older age, the bullying escalates in no time to serious violence, dangerous enough to warrant police involvement. Adult intervention is crucial to keep adolescents out of the courts and out of hospital.

Most important, though, is the fact that the victim needs to know he has a right not to be bullied and the right to be protected from harm. All too often the victim adopts the attitude that he has done something to deserve the mistreatment.

HOW SIBLINGS CAN HELP

While a victim's parents may be completely unaware of the bullying, a sibling (who may have seen the action on the bus or in the playground) often knows long before anyone else. How they respond can make or break the bully cycle. Some advice to pass on to family members to help them protect each other:

- Talk to your brother or sister about what you've noticed, and try to get him or her to tell a grown-up.
- Offer to speak to a grown-up yourself. Promise to do your best to keep the reporting secret.
- If you feel confident enough, tell the bully that you know what's going on and will not sit back and let it happen. Don't use your fists to fight him. Use your head.
- Raise the issue of bullying in general with your friends or classmates. Try to get discussions going so that they might examine their own consciences and experiences. You may even raise the idea of classroom discussions with your teacher.

Most boys wouldn't dare tell their fathers; they don't want to let them down. They have a "manly" image to live up to and it doesn't include weakness. How many times were they told "big boys don't cry"? They've never seen daddy cry, have they?

Fathers can reassure their sons by letting them know that victimization is not a sign of failure, that fear and sadness are not wimpy emotions and that being bullied is not their fault.

Above all, whether it is a son or a daughter who has confided the truth about a bullying problem, he or she should be congratulated. The victim has shown great courage to step out of silent suffering. Now is the time for some major reassurance. Tell your child that you know bullying feels rotten, that it is not her fault, and that she is not alone—you are there to help. She also needs to know that adults take the matter seriously, that she will be protected, the bully dealt with and steps taken to ensure it does not happen again.

Now it's your turn, mom and dad. Your child has told you someone has been bullying him. The ball is in your court and it's very important how you play it. You must be committed to following through.

PARENTS' CRUCIAL FIRST RESPONSE

Margaret has four children in public school. A stay-at-home mom who does volunteer work in the school, she found that her high profile among the students helped her to help Susie, her 13-year-old daughter.

On her way home from school the bullies took regular pleasure in pushing Susie into the snow bank and strewing her homework around the road and sidewalks. Margaret suggested that Susie try to avoid the bullies by waiting after school until they had left. But poor Susie didn't want to hang around the school all alone. Finally Margaret hit upon a solution: she approached the bullies and offered to walk them home from school. She told them, "If you're having difficulties behaving yourselves like good citizens, then I'd be happy to help you do that." And because she was a regular presence in the school, she says, they seemed to be a little more compliant. Every day after school, she and her dog walked the bullies home from school. Now it has become a kind of amusing tradition. The bullies vie for the privilege of walking the dog and the harassment of her daughter has ended.

To what degree should a parent become involved? Margaret leapt right in and for her it worked. It's not an approach that would work for everyone. Rather, it's the attitude behind the action that works. Margaret knew this was not child's play; the bullying was traumatic for Susie and merited her full attention. When someone is power-tripping on your child, you don't leave him to fight his own battles; you listen with respect and then work together, parent and child, to extricate him from the mess. By stepping forward and trying to change the situation, you are modelling assertiveness for your child.

Picture yourself in that situation. If you were regularly confronted with another adult assaulting you or attempting extortion, you would know it was illegal and would probably know what courses of action were available to you, but you would still be pretty shaken up. Just imagine how much worse it is for a child who knows nothing about legalities and what resources are out there to help her, yet is faced with this threat on a daily basis. (It may just be her lunch money, but it is extortion nonetheless.) That's why it is imperative, when a child consults you, you give him or her your serious attention.

It's important, too, to keep in mind your own prejudices. Some parents have had their own painful experiences when young and are more anxious about bullying. They may transmit their lack of confidence to their child. If you find yourself panicking on your child's behalf, remind yourself to put aside your own emotional baggage and show a calm, confident attitude.

First, remember that your child may want more than anything else simply to unload.

> *"I really needed someone to talk to," a Grade 9 student says, remembering the bullying she went through in elementary school. "If I talked to my dad, I felt he really didn't want to hear about it. He would say, 'We'll do this and this' or 'We'll talk to the parents' or 'Just hit him back' or 'Go tell the principal'—all these things we should do, as if he wanted to deal with the problem and get it out of the way. But my mom just sat and listened to me. That really helped. I needed to talk and I didn't have any friends I could tell."*

Talking is a great help. But when bullying gets to the point where the child obviously can't handle it alone, where he doesn't want to go to school and may be complaining of tummy aches to stay at home, then it may be time to contact the teacher. In most cases, children don't have it in their power to stop a bully. Expecting them to fight their own battles is an adult cop-out.

Although your child will probably try to persuade you to stay quiet about the problem, this may be one time that you should ignore him and air his dirty laundry. Teachers may not be aware of the bullying problem and, if they don't know, they can't help. Begin with the teacher and work your way up the hierarchy until you hear a satisfactory response. Ask your child if he would like to join you in the meeting; it may make him feel more in control. Don't march in on an angry mission. Approach the school diplomatically. "We have a problem," you could say. "How can we help solve it?" Talk to the school staff as inconspicuously as possible; ask them to promise some form of confidentiality and protection. You could, for example, persuade teachers to "catch" the bully in the act so that it does not look like your child has snitched. The school may also need to rearrange school-bus transportation routes or keep the bully after school until the other students have gone. Both parents and teachers need to work together to stop bullying and to deal with the harasser as swiftly and seriously as possible. In fact a growing number of educators and child development experts say charges should be laid whenever possible, particularly when a child has been threatened or injured.

> *"It tears your heart out," says one father, who is also an elementary-school vice-principal. "My son went through it for two years, and every night was a fight, trying to persuade him to go to school the next day. You've just got to get in there and fight for your kid; you've got to let the school know."*

If you've never been an activist before, now is the time to speak out, make a polite fuss. Tell the teacher or principal you will phone back the next day to see how things are going. If the principal promises to deal with the problem and nothing happens, persevere. Hound the school if you have to, but be warned: you may be dismissed as an over-protective parent. Although attitudes are beginning to change, there are still a few, even among educators, who believe that "boys will be boys."

If the school is not terribly attentive, you may need to sleuth a bit to find out if other parents have had similar bully troubles. Try saying to other parents "We've been experiencing some trouble with one of the kids at school. Have you?" There's strength in numbers and it may bolster your case if the troublemaker has been making trouble with others. The parent really shouldn't have to do this kind of scrambling—the school should be ready to do whatever it takes to ensure students are safe—but if you have to, you have to. Besides, finding other children in the same boat can help your child feel less isolated. And he will be less likely to be singled out by the bully for retaliation.

Some parents have marched over to the bully's parents to vent their anger and enlist the other family's aid in stopping the bad behavior. But that can be disappointing, dangerous even. Not everyone shares the same view of bullying.

Twelve-year-old John bulldozed his way through his small-town elementary school. He threw snow in a teaching assistant's face, hit another in the chest, fought continually with his classmates and swore at his teachers. The school tried suspending him, over and over again, but nothing improved. It didn't help that John's parents were backing him up all the way. The situation turned from bad to worse and now John's parents are suing the school staff for unjustly suspending him. They told a school board meeting that the school is harassing their son and plotting to get him kicked out. John showed up at the meeting wearing a T-shirt emblazoned with the slogan "Kick Butt."

This is not the kind of family you can expect to sit down over tea and discuss bullying in a civilized manner. Unless you know the parents really well, it may not be a good idea to independently air your concerns with the bully's family. They may be proud of their little one's "spunk" or they may be bullies themselves. Some schools have found that in some circumstances it helps to bring together the parents of the bully and victim to discuss the problem. But that's not always the case. One school-board psychologist remembers arranging a meeting between the victim and the bully's parents that ended with the dads slugging it out in the restaurant lobby. Emotions sometimes run too high in bullying issues to risk face-to-face encounters.

That's why parent education is such an important part of any anti-bullying campaign. The bully's parents may be unaware of the problem or hold totally different attitudes. Encourage the school to involve the bully and her parents in the solution. It may be helpful to ask the school to set up a parenting network or discussion group to explore ideas for stopping bullying at home and school. This way the bully's parents can have their eyes opened a bit without blame. All parents need to recognize when bullying is happening and why it should be stopped.

If the bullying continues despite your efforts at a cooperative solution, ask school administrators to transfer the bully to another classroom or even to another school. Failing that, you may want to transfer your own child to

TIPS FOR PARENTS

- Give your children every chance possible to be healthy with proper nutrition, sleep and exercise. A healthy child is better able to cope with the stresses of childhood social experiences.
- Encourage her to remember her strong points when someone calls her names. If someone is calling her dumb, teach her to say out-loud, or to herself, "I am definitely not dumb. I am a great piano player, or, I get great marks in writing class."
- Encourage independence. You want a child who is self-reliant, not awaiting adult rescue from every difficulty.
- Talk with your child about why she thinks she is being bullied. Remind her that everyone feels left out at some time.
- Teach him to ignore the laughter of others. The giggles can be as damaging as the bully's actions.
- If your child is regularly excluded from a clique, sympathize and ask him what he can do to make himself feel better. Ask him who is *not* being mean to him. If he notices that some kids are nice, he can work on building a friendship with them; one-on-one playdates on his own turf may boost his self-confidence. But don't let him continually bang his head against a brick wall: if certain kids are rejecting him, show him how to reject them first. Do this by providing a more appealing playtime activity—maybe send him to school with a tennis ball or yo-yo and encourage him to invite other, nicer kids to play, rather than continue to push for acceptance from the unfriendly group.
- If the bullying is happening on the bus or on the walk to and from school, arrange for a socially strong older student to accompany him or find an alternative method of transportation until the situation is resolved.
- Ask him: "What is the bully trying to make you feel?" Get him to think about what happens if he shows those feelings.
- Suggest she invite friends over for dinner or on an outing,

and do your best to ensure the experience is a pleasant one.

- Increase family discussion of feelings. Show your child how to let other people know how he or she is feeling.
- If your child seems socially immature, offer opportunities for social interaction. He may benefit from buddying up with someone who is younger and on the same level of social development. Arrange for them to play in simple, non-threatening ways, in quiet activities at home. He can gradually move on to more challenging situations as he stores up a memory of positive experiences.
- Investigate the possibility of setting up a parents group to discuss and brainstorm ways of solving the bullying problem.
- Talk to the teacher about the problem if your child is being isolated. He or she may be able to rearrange desks to break up a domineering clique, use more co-operative learning approaches, or pair your child with another potential friend on a class project.
- Compliment your child's appearance and praise him, realistically and specifically, whenever you can. Try to arrange situations in which he can do something well, preferably when other children are around to see.
- Help him to recognize and avoid humiliating or vulnerable situations by talking about a variety of possible scenarios.

a new school. Or, if you think the situation is serious enough, and if the school is not handling it to your satisfaction, move up the political ranks with your complaint; threaten to use the media if action is not taken. It may even be necessary to contact the police. Get legal advice to see where you stand. Some parents have gone to the extent of suing the school, administrators and the board of education for failing to protect their child. In Forsyth, Georgia, a fifth-grader complained for six months that a male classmate was groping and sexually taunting her.

Despite being told of eight such incidents, teachers and the principal did nothing, so her mother took them to court. The U.S. Supreme Court ruled that, while damages were not available for "simple acts of teasing and name-calling," schools may be held liable for ignoring severe sexual harassment among students. This may be a confrontational way of solving the problem, but backing your kid to the very end and using the legal system to protect the innocent can teach your child some valuable lessons.

LOOKING AHEAD: BEHAVIOR PROBLEMS THAT INVITE BULLYING AND WHAT YOU CAN DO TO HELP

Once the bullying incident is in the past, it's time to look closely at your child to see what it is about him that is leaving him open to attack. His looks or behavior, quirky and dear as they are to you, may be inviting the bully's attention. A gentle makeover might be in order.

But is that fair? Isn't it putting the onus in the wrong place, expecting an innocent victim to change his ways? It's a little like telling a raped woman she should stop wearing miniskirts.

It may not be fair at all. But if you are a parent, you are probably ready to do whatever it takes to stop your child's pain. And for some children whose looks or actions don't fit the norm, this may be what it takes.

You could try switching schools. This may or may not be successful. Bully expert Dan Olweus has found that victimization ends when the victim is older and is able to choose his own social and physical environments. The same can be true if children themselves are part of the decision to transfer to another school.

But for some children, this doesn't work. They seem to

be incapable of shaking the role as victim. Their parents might move them to a new school because of bullying but within three weeks they're being picked on by bullies at the new school.

It's a fact: some kids are simply a magnet for maliciousness. They send out signals of "victimidity," a kind of red flag that invites the bully to charge. Being smaller than average doesn't help, especially if you're a boy, but it doesn't necessarily doom a child to victimization and it obviously isn't a characteristic that can be changed. But negative body language can attract bullying and can be changed.

Lack of eye contact, gaze aversion, withdrawal in conflict are some of the unspoken signals than can make a shy child appear frightened, cautious or submissive. Bullies who are hunting down victims look for those signals in their classmates. You can look for them, too, in your own child.

Here are some adjustments you can make to your child's appearance and actions so he or she will seem less open to attack:

- Non-conformity definitely makes a child noticeable. One boy stuck out like a sore thumb because his mom gave him an atrocious haircut. Keep tabs on what's considered "in" and "out" and make sure your child's clothes and hairstyles fit in with the crowd. Do this within reason. You may not be able to—or want to—spend $200 on top-of-the-line sneakers, but there may be room for compromise. You don't necessarily want to discourage non-conformity either. Some kids prefer to march to the beat of their own drummer. Discuss the issue with your child and let him be your guide.

- Just because you coped with crooked teeth doesn't mean your child should. A strong character may help a child survive a small deformity. But if your child is suffering and you can do something about it—orthodontic work, for example—it may be worth the cost. Your child's self-esteem may get a big boost.

- Does your child make weak retaliatory threats in response to teasing? A bully can't resist that; it seems to egg him on. Teach your child that a closed mouth may have more impact than one that spouts off ineffectively. Explain, for example, that if the bully runs off with his hat, the worst thing he can do is chase after him. Better that he calmly tell the bully he wants it back but will not chase him. Remind your child that if his belongings are damaged or stolen, an adult can always help him later. Teach him not to argue with a bully's remarks; if what is being said about him is untrue, it's better to say something short and simple, like "maybe" and walk away.

- If his social skills need work, if his behavior stands out in any way when he is with his peers, the bully will hone in on him. The child with this kind of difficulty may need extra coaching. One 11-year-old boy with learning disabilities, for example, had to be taught to offer chocolate to other children if he was eating some in front of them.

- If your children have obvious differences or physical disabilities that can't be changed, you should do your best to make them comfortable with them. It can help to point out successful people with the same problem: Michael J. Fox and his short stature, for example, or Einstein and his learning disabilities. But choose your role models carefully and don't belabor the point. (My parents tried to make me feel better about the size of my nose by pointing out that Barbra Streisand had a big nose too. That made things worse. I thought Streisand was funny-looking. I didn't want to look like her; I wanted to look like Olivia Newton-John.)

After you have pinpointed some of the more obvious problems and tried to alleviate them, it may help to involve your child in a sports program where he can learn to feel comfortable with his body. Even as some rapists will avoid attacking a person who walks with a sense of purpose, so body self-confidence helps avoid sending a message of timidity. Unfortunately, in this day and age it may be difficult for a boy heavily involved in the arts. Our cultural prejudices are too entrenched. A boy is valued more by many in our society if he is physically coordinated and fit. But artistic ability can be tactfully directed; a boy who is artistically inclined may garner the respect of his peers if he can build a fabulous go-cart or tree house. And any child who can swing the bat with purpose, swim a mean backstroke, perfect a pirouette or master a horse, for example, seems to carry himself or herself a little differently, with a little more pride.

But don't get your child so obsessively involved in a sport that it takes him away from the mainstream and interferes with social or family life. Minor-league hockey is notorious for that. The best approach is a pleasant, stimulating balance of activities. Pick a sport geared to your child's personality type. You may love the idea of your son as Wayne Gretzky, but if he's shy and quiet, hockey may not be his thing. Swimming or baseball may be better bets. And pick the coach carefully too. Ask other parents for their recommendations and watch the coach in action. Is he right in there with the kids, sensitive to tiny egos and a nurturer of self-esteem? He should be considerate of all team members, not so keen to win that he becomes a bully himself.

> *Ten-year-old Annie was always at the bottom rung of the social ladder in her class. Most of her social problems stemmed from her learning disability and a poor academic performance. Her already fragile self-esteem was further battered by a younger brother who was exceptionally bright.*
>
> *But Annie has recently become involved in Girl Guides and her mother says it's done wonders. Not only have they discovered Annie's hidden talent— she has a flair for arts and crafts—but she has learned a lot about the give-and-take necessary to build successful social relationships and has made her first really close friend. It seems to have given Annie a fresh, confident new look at life.*

Social skills are incredibly important during the childhood years and some children seem to come upon them a little more easily than others. If your child is being bullied, she may need a gentle social boost. Experts suggest the following:

- Give children time, space and encouragement to develop their talents.
- Be a matchmaker. Help them make friends, with the popular children if possible. Ask the child's teacher who may be the best bet for a friend for your child, then set up a play date or outing. For young children

especially, make sure you're in close proximity when they're together to help guide the friendship and smooth over any bumpy spots.

- Teach them in detail how to make friends: give them good opening lines to start a conversation, point out the value in getting others to talk about themselves and talk to them about praise, consideration and the give-and-take that is part of every friendship.

- Encourage them to look outside themselves and at the world around them, to develop a wider interest in what others are doing. (Shy children are often overly concerned about the effect they are having on others.)

- Wherever possible, point out to them how other people may be feeling. This encourages them to look outwards, develop empathy and an appreciation for the other child's viewpoint.

- Role-playing can be a great tool for teaching skills like listening and negotiating. Some children may need a little extra practice reading non-verbal messages and handling emotions. Try acting out different situations and then discussing options for behavior. At home, you can also use your child's relationships with siblings to teach sharing and cooperation.

- Read and talk about bully stories or some of the classic "under-dog" books like *The Ugly Duckling*, *Tortoise and the Hare* or *The Little Engine that Could*. (See Resource section for more ideas.)

- Teasing—when it is done in good fun—can help "toughen up" an overly sensitive child and encourage a sense of humor. Among family members or between close friends, it can be a sign of a strong relationship. It is important, however, to enforce a family rule: teasing is only allowed if both parties are enjoying it. If someone wants it to stop, stop. Teach your child to say "I don't think that's funny" and to respect it when others say so. For an extra-sensitive child, or one who is dealing with other stressful issues, even light-hearted teasing can hurt. When teasing becomes mean, it becomes bullying.

- Sometimes, however, a child's social behavior can be such a problem that you may be better off seeking outside help from a school guidance counsellor or child psychologist.

COACHING A GOOD COMEBACK

Tommy was a pudgy little boy with a big problem. The big kids liked to tease him and call him names like "chubbo." When they did, Tommy whimpered. Then his parents helped him create and practice a different response. Now he gives them a good comeback like "More of me to love!" It's given his predicament a lighter tone and given Tommy a feeling of empowerment. The bullies don't bug him as much any more.

Bullying rarely begins with blows; it usually starts out verbally, with teasing or name-calling. The more compliant and fearful the victim appears, the more satisfied the bully is. The bully must have loved Tommy's whimpering. Giving him that power whetted his appetite and made him hungry for more. The bully often counts on seeing his victim cower right away. That's why a surprising, creative or funny comeback can sometimes work.

Bryce has had some real problems at school. He has a learning disability—a social-behavior deficit that causes him to speak too loudly and inappropriately—and some of his unusual mannerisms make him stand out in class. His classmates tease him continually "just 'cause I talk too much. I feel kind of left out. I'm always crying after school. It's because of my learning disability. I didn't do anything bad."

Although he is still having some problems getting along with others, the bullying has been eased by his taking lessons in social skills. The classes, which were aimed at children with learning disabilities,[3] taught him to lay the blame for bullying not on himself but on the other children who can't accept differences. "I know now that it's not my problem; it's theirs," he says. He has learned some good comebacks too: "Like when they say, 'You're one big chicken with nice long wings,' I say, 'What you say bounces off me and sticks on you.' Or if they call me a chicken, I say, 'What do you want, a wing or a leg?'"

Research shows that the more ideas a child has about handling social situations, the better his or her social adjustment is. Role-playing can give children those ideas. It has worked well in helping them say no to drugs and sexual abuse. A similar approach can be just as successful in dealing with bullying.

Try acting out a typical bullying episode and see what kinds of approaches your child can come up with. He may surprise you. Kids can think up solutions that adults would never dream of. If your child's creative juices aren't flowing, you may suggest your own ideas and help him rehearse them. If possible, have him practice with siblings. What you hope to do with this ad-lib rec-room theater is give him tools with which he can better handle an attack—and maybe get him to laugh about it a bit, give him a lighter, healthier attitude towards the problem.

Remember that some children need to be taught about subtlety. Remind her not to try her comeback in front of a teacher, for example, or she may find herself knee-deep in trouble of a different kind. Help her learn how not to goad the bully into putting her fists where her mouth is; chances are good the bully will. One student remembers telling a bully who was picking on a smaller child, "Why don't you pick on someone your own size?" The bully did; he reached out and threw the would-be hero across the room. A good comeback must be non-hostile and subtle enough not to provoke more trouble.

THE BENEFITS OF MARTIAL ARTS TRAINING

Terrence was a big kid, so big that he couldn't fight and he couldn't run fast. Dickie and Vinnie knew it and they loved it. They'd throw him to the ground with their knees on his arms, pinning him down, making him do things he didn't want to. Terrence didn't cry, but he didn't fight back either.

One day Dickie had captured him in the neighbor's yard when Terrence was suddenly stung in the back by a bee. He leaped up off the ground and his sheer bulk threw Dickie across the yard. Dickie lay there, stunned. It was a moment of truth: both boys realized then and there that

Terrence was actually stronger. Dickie never beat him up again.

What broke that bullying cycle was Terrence and Dickie's sudden knowledge that Terrence didn't have to be a victim. This knowledge took away some of the fear for Terrence, and gave him confidence to face his opposition. And he says that, because he wasn't afraid, he knew he didn't have to fight back; the knowledge of his strength made him strong.

A surprising show of strength can throw a curve at the bully and give the victim a chance to slip away unscathed. It doesn't have to be a display of physical strength. It can be confidence or an "attitude" of strength. For some children, self-defence training may be the answer. Proponents of self-defence and the martial arts say that simply knowing you can protect yourself can keep you from being victimized. It is not the physical use of the training, they say, but the change in attitude that results. A child who knows she can protect herself if she really has to no longer views herself as a victim and she can face the bully head-on, passing on to him an unmistakable message of self-confidence and assertiveness.

Terrence now has his doctorate degree in psychology, a fifth-degree black belt in karate and has studied martial arts for more than 30 years. He is convinced that martial-arts training can give students the same knowledge of strength that his bee-sting incident gave him years ago.

Other psychologists and educators agree. Many parents have tried enrolling their children in the self-defence classes with the hope that their children will become newly assertive.

But there is a danger in this. Martial-arts training may

exacerbate a bullying problem if the victim starts to believe he is so tough that he can turn the tables and beat up others. Sometimes a child can feel obligated to fight: "Now that I've got a black belt, I've got to stand up to them."

Using martial arts for self-defence in real life is dangerous. A student of Karate or Tae Kwon Do has learned his skills by practicing on mats on the floor with another child who is programmed to fight in the same way. Street fights don't work that way; the scrappers usually end up wrestling on the ground in a dirty free-for-all. And those impressive martial-arts brick-strikers are often lousy fist-fighters. Performers who can smash a bare hand through a stack of bricks are trained to use the first two knuckles of their fingers and their technique only works on a flat surface, says Wally Slocki, a founder of Superkids, an educational center that teaches children martial arts. In a real fight, Slocki adds, it is usually the last three knuckles that get used. You may look good on stage, but you could get walloped in the playground.

Slocki says he counsels karate students at Superkids that their best defence is not offence; that it's better to high-tail it out of there and tell an adult than to try a karate chop on the bully. He also suggests that martial-arts teachers encourage kids to talk about conflict and practice role-playing to teach them how to solve a problem before it becomes physical. A good martial arts course won't consist of kicking and punching and learning how to be like Bruce Lee but instead will involve lots of reading, philosophy, discipline and social-skills training.

Unfortunately, instructors of martial arts are often high-school kids pumped full of hormones, not well-grounded in the gentle philosophy behind martial arts. For this reason, a properly coached sports team may be better for building sportsmanship, character and self-confidence.

And if he encounters a gang or group of teenage swarmers, even the best trained Karate Kid is going to get clobbered, police say. Dealing with a mob of bullies is a different matter altogether.

SURVIVING THE GROUP BULLY ATTACK

One mother recounts how her 15-year-old son was swarmed by a group of teenage bullies. "We were told later by friends that if he had appeared more aggressive or if he had done this or done that, he could have prevented it, but I think basically he didn't have a chance."

Police tend to agree. There's not much a young person can do when accosted by an aggressive group of children who are high on their own power. Forget the karate kicks and snappy comebacks. A group bully requires a different response.

In a swarming situation, there are five possible defences a young person may follow:

1. Fight back—now, or later with friends.
2. Run.
3. Yell for help.
4. Tell a grownup.
5. Bow down and take it.

Police have some depressing news: none of these options really works. Surveys show that most young people choose revenge: if they get swarmed, they go back and get their friends. But police say this approach leads to escalating violence that quite often doesn't end until someone gets badly hurt or killed.

Fighting back with a group of bullies is another dumb move, even if the youth thinks he's safe because he has a knife in his pocket. In one survey, more than half of the teenagers questioned said they carried knives for protection. But police maintain that, when a victim pulls out a knife, it gets used on the victim virtually every time.3 The presence of a weapon tends to rev up the crowd and the outnumbered victim often loses his grip; the weapon slips out of his hand. Even if the victim does get a chance to use the knife to protect himself, he is the one who will be charged.

If your child shouldn't fight back, then what about option number two? Should your child run? If he does, he had better outrun all 15 bullies, because if they catch him they're going to be *really* pumped and ready to pummel.

What about yelling? That doesn't always work, either. The fear of getting involved seems to halt any potential Good Samaritans in their tracks. Metro Toronto Police Detective Sergeant Steve Duggan tells of incidents like the time a young person was pushed in front of a subway train with scores of witnesses—yet no one came to his rescue; and of a bus driver driving away even though a machete was being taken to a youth on the sidewalk.

Option number four, tattling on the group, can also lead to more trouble. Often the child is afraid to tell his parents. If he was bullied by a gang outside his favorite hangout, there is a fear his parents will grill him on his whereabouts: "What were you doing in that end of town anyway?" They may even ground him, forbid him from hanging out there any more. Then he has to tell his friends he's not allowed to go out with them and he looks like a wimp. If the incident occurs at school, he could try risking his reputation among his classmates and tell the teacher. But the teacher may just shake his head in frustration because dealing with discipline problems has become a fruitless, thankless task. Or he may march the bullies down to the principal's office where they get a reprimand and a "slap on the wrist": very little incentive not to do it again and great incentive to get revenge.

> Mark, a quiet, shy 15-year-old boy who did well in his Vancouver-area school, failed to observe the one rule that could provide protection against the group bully attack: he was seen alone.
>
> This boy who rarely got into trouble is in trouble now. A life-endangering kind of trouble in the intensive care unit. Unconscious, on life-sustaining apparatus, he may never know what he did wrong. But one night on the way home from a babysitting job, he made the mistake of being alone and looking alone. A group of teens leaving a party descended on him. They threw him onto the sidewalk, placed his arm against the curb and took turns stomping on it. After the fun was over, Mark had a fractured skull, humerus and ribs, and if he ever recovers consciousness, he will be permanently brain-damaged.

Once again, the best defence is avoidance. Kids have always wanted to be popular; today, it's a survival skill. As a parent, it's a good idea to encourage your child's friendships, ideally with those kids who seem to have high morals and two feet on the ground. The smart kids are the ones with lots of friends and with a reputation for having lots of friends. Your child won't be messed with if he doesn't look like a solitary sitting duck. It is a shame that childhood must become so defensive. But in many towns and cities, this is a teenage fact of life.

TIP FOR SWARMING VICTIMS

Parents can pass this advice on to their teens if they are worried about potential gang problems:

- If you find yourself in a swarming situation, scream "Fire!" as loudly as you can. It sounds silly, but police say it works because people will run to investigate or call 911. They may ignore you if you yell for help. Make it a self-confident yell to let the bullies know you're strong and safe and not to be messed with. Practice at home and make it come from the gut.

Surviving a bout with a bully is not simply a question of fight or flight. There are other, better options. Your role as parent is to help your children create their own alternatives and coach them on their use. You may want to help them modify their behavior, improve their social skills, build their self-confidence so that they are well-armed for the next encounter. Then it's your job to marshall the adult forces in your children's world to see to it that the bullying stops. And your prime partner in this battle is probably your child's school.

6

Helping the Victim:
The School's Role

Tammy's favorite pastime was bullying the other girls in her high school. After one particularly bad incident, the school suspended her. When she returned to class, the principal met with her and her parents to try to work out a contract to change her behavior. He suggested an anger-management course. Her parents reacted with considerable anger of their own. Their daughter didn't need that kind of help. And so the bullying continued. Not long after that, she attacked another girl in the cafeteria and several teachers had to pull her away. The school called the police, who laid charges. Her parents were furious. "Why did you do that?" they asked the principal. "Why didn't you just suspend her again?"

It's the kind of incident that makes school authorities throw their hands up in frustration. School is the place

126

where most bullying occurs, yet teachers face tremendous odds if they want to make a dent in the problem, especially when their primary partners, the parents, aren't on the same wavelength.

Teachers today are overloaded. They are expected to be psychologists, police, social workers and still teach the three Rs. They are expected to fix what's wrong with society and the economy. On top of that, they often have to counteract troubled parenting and deal tactfully with moms and dads who are uncertain or hyper-sensitive about their role.

Parent-teacher conferences on a bully problem can be tricky. In an ideal situation, both parents and teachers are pulling together to help the kids. But it doesn't always work that way. Often conference turns into confrontation. Teachers tiptoe through a minefield of emotions, knowing that to criticize a child is to appear to criticize the parents as well.

Sometimes parents resent the implied criticism of their parenting skills and defensively rush to their children's rescue. Others feel that the school is picking on their child because he or she belongs to a particular minority group. Or the parent may be a single mother, unemployed or economically frazzled; facing yet another problem is just asking too much. Some parents carry bad memories of bullies they encountered in their own school days and this affects how they handle their child's difficulties. In today's schools, with their medley of cultures, prejudices and values, it is a tall order to impose uniform standards of behavior.

But if a bullying problem is going to be solved, parents and teachers must collaborate. It helps if parents have an idea of the kind of pressures teachers face today.

STORMS AND STRESS IN THE CLASSROOM

You hear it in teacher staff rooms everywhere: schools have changed. Those good old Golden Rule days have tarnished. More and more, reading, 'riting and 'rithmetic are being shoved aside by scuffles, squabbles and emotional emergencies.

A survey of 17,000 Canadian teachers released in 1992[1] found that teachers are increasingly concerned about students' behavior and their own rate of burn-out. The teachers, surveyed by researchers from Queen's University, believe that the increase in television-watching, childhood freedom, single-parent families, immigrants and special-needs children has stirred up such a turbulence in the classroom that everyone—teachers and kids alike—is stressed out.

Most of the teachers surveyed said that today's students are more aggressive, more argumentative and more likely to display social and behavioral problems at school than ever before. Maintaining discipline, they said, takes an inordinate amount of time—time that could be better spent teaching.

Bullying and aggressive behavior in general are the hot topics among educators. Everywhere, schools are scrambling to find ways to defuse the violence, from the gentle approaches—counselling and therapy—to the not-so-gentle—metal detectors and police patrolling the hallway.

And on the front lines, weary teachers are calling for help. There is a crisis in childhood aggression, they say, and teachers should be better trained to deal with it. But teachers are also up against pressure from the taxpaying public and parents concerned about "The Basics." These are high-pressure, high-profile groups that complain schools spend too much time on so-called frills, trying to socialize children at the expense of the three Rs. And they don't like teachers assuming the role traditionally taken by parents or social agencies.

Barbara Whitehead called it the "psychologizing of education." In her *Atlantic Monthly* article[2] she wrote: "The curriculum is becoming more therapeutic: children are taking courses in self-esteem, conflict resolution and aggression management. Parental advisory groups are conscientiously debating alternative approaches to traditional school discipline.... Schools are increasingly becoming emergency rooms of the emotions."

Parent or taxpayer, you can't help but wonder: is it any of the schools' business who is bullying whom?

THE BULLY'S STOMPING GROUND

Bullying *is* the school's business. It must be: the school provides the locale, the audience, maybe even the atmosphere that's conducive to bullying. The fact is, school is where most childhood bullying takes place. And when discipline is not handled firmly and consistently, the playground and corridors can be hotbeds of hotheads.

Schools are pretty aggressive places. When researcher Debra Pepler videotaped activity in two school playgrounds, she was astounded to uncover a bullying episode on average every seven-and-a-half minutes. Every few minutes somebody took a power trip at somebody else's expense; several times each recess, some child experienced terror, pain or humiliation. And in 3.6 per cent of the cases, students used knives, skipping ropes and balls as weapons. These are elementary-school kids. And they're armed.

As one shell-shocked student put it, with a simple, succinct little shrug: "You always have to watch your back." She doesn't say this in a complaining way. For her, and others, this is a fact of life.

Research shows the most common location for bullying is in the playground. The worst places are where there is competition for limited resources: play equipment, goal posts, even the school wall.[3]

What is most alarming, though, is that bullying is often not hidden away in some dark corner far from public view. Studies show that supervised settings, such as classrooms and hallways, are twice as likely to be hot spots for bullies than unsupervised settings, such as on the way to and from school. And bullying is more likely to occur close to the school building—within 120 feet— than in parts of the playground that are farther away.[4]

In one study in which respondents could check more than one alternative, researchers found that bullying happens in the following locations:

- 81 percent reported bullying occurs in the playground;
- 57 percent said it happened in hallways;
- 50 percent said it happened in classrooms;
- 37 percent said it happened in lunchrooms;
- 35 percent said it happened on the way home from school;
- 28 percent said it happened in washrooms;
- 25 percent said it happened on the way to school.[5]

Although the data are still scant, it appears that the amount of bullying has little to do with how big or small the school is, or with how many students are in a class, though there may be more bullying in single-sex rather than mixed-sex schools.[6] And the jury is still out on the issue of neighborhood and school location. Most researchers say bullying occurs just as frequently in small towns and rural areas as it does in big cities.

At any rate, whether you live in a small town or a big city, you can be sure the bullies are out there, getting their kicks on a daily basis. And right now some child, somewhere, is living in fear.

All this aggression can't help but affect learning. Experts say it does. Bullies face an uncertain academic future. Victims' education may also be disrupted when their school days are soured by fear. Concern for safety can make concentration tough, inhibit participation in group learning activities and may even keep the child away from school with feigned or psychosomatic illnesses.

And while the bullies' and victims' education suffers, the rest of the students are getting lessons of a different sort—lessons we don't want them to receive.

LESSONS IN AGGRESSION

"Our younger son was in the eighth grade when he was attacked by three boys on the way home from school," one mother recounts. "He escaped by going into a neighbor's house. When my husband complained to the school principal about the matter, he was evasive and uncooperative. When I called the other parents of kids in the class, only one father was cooperative. After that I complained to our MP, MPP and school trustee, but all of them said there was nothing they could do. Later I mentioned this to another school trustee and she brushed it off as too trivial to even give it a second thought. Several weeks ago we

> *went to a meeting of a political party's local*
> *riding and again mentioned it to one of the*
> *women. She dismissed it, saying, 'Everyone gets*
> *beaten up once in a while.' "*

What kind of message does this tolerance of violence give our children? A bully's reign of terror affects the whole school, and when it's ignored or downplayed children learn that might means right. They learn that if they can't be the bully, then they'd better be on the bully's side. Or if they can't do that, then they'd best keep their mouths shut.

Experts say schools must take responsibility for who is bullying whom. It may not be easy, coming in so late in the game. Much of a bully's bad behavior has probably been cemented outside the classroom in his early developing years, and once a child enters school those deeply ingrained personality problems are tough to correct. In fact, some child psychologists say a child's behavior is set and predictable as early as Grades 1 or 2. But the school system can make a difference, using better vigilance and consistent consequences, in ensuring that bullying does not occur on their property.

Dr. Dan Olweus goes even further. He believes it is a fundamental societal responsibility to put an end to childhood bullying. It is up to adults—be they teachers, parents or lawmakers—to prevent and intervene in bullying problems because, Olweus says, it is the democratic right of every child to be spared this denigrating treatment.

Unfortunately, there has been considerable pressure brought to bear on schools to discourage them from dealing with the problem.

ROADBLOCKS TO REFORM

The school bully had just finished having a go at one of the children in his school and was turning to leave. "I'm telling my mom on you," his battered victim cried. The bully had a quick response for that: "If you tell your mom, I'll sue you."

Out of the mouths of babes and bullies comes the most astonishing stuff, remarks that can tell us a lot about ourselves and the society in which we live.

Concern over lawsuits and civil rights, ignorance, fear and political correctness all conspire to keep the bully firmly ensconced atop his pedestal. North American society has been inadvertently sheltering the bully: from the local principal keeping his mouth shut because he is reluctant to criminalize a child, all the way up to federal laws that protect the young offender.

In recent years zero-tolerance policies and codes of behavior have given some discipline power back to schools, but old habits are hard to break. Some school administrators still hesitate to involve outside authorities in dealing with bullying, clinging to the old belief that a victim will be a victim until she learns to fight back. Others have chosen to sweep bully brouhahas under the carpet, or deal with them quietly on their own, in order to safeguard their school's reputation. Some principals don't want to risk the implication that there is anything wrong with their school. They worry that making a fuss about bully problems will hurt their image and enrolment, so they opt for the least conspicuous damage control possible. Across North America there are increasing demands, from those concerned about educational standards, for more private-enterprise-like competition among public schools. Some educators fear that competition for students could encourage more such cover-ups.

This kind of insensitivity to the plight of the victim has pushed some frustrated parents to the extreme of selling their home, moving to a new neighborhood and switching their children's school after several years of bullying with no action by the school.

The concern over individual human rights has also, ironically, thwarted efforts to crack down on the bully. Some say the pendulum has swung too far in favor of children's rights and left teachers hogtied. Today the bully and his family are more likely to challenge authorities head-on, and administrators may be paralyzed by fear of legalities.

The Queen's University study found that, since the implementation of the Canadian Charter of Rights and Freedoms and the Young Offenders' Act, teachers feel they have even less authority to discipline students or to defend themselves from unjust accusations. As one high-school teacher said, "In the halls you think twice about getting involved in some instances because teachers' rights are not as protected as students' rights."

Another Grade 6 teacher told the researchers, "It seems whatever approach we take to discipline, we have been abusive or infringed on someone's civil rights. Kids today know this."

Young people are well-versed on their rights and the Young Offenders Act. In Canada, children under age 12 can't be charged with any crime. That's why two boys in Regina, who recently chained an eight- and a nine-year-old boy to the roof of a downtown office building and then beat them and sexually assaulted them for seven hours, got off scot-free. The boys, known by many as the neighborhood bullies, were eight and 11 years old and therefore couldn't be charged. Many children realize exactly what they can and can't get away with and it has given these mini-manipulators a feeling of immunity.

Teachers complain that aggressive children are often backed up by rights-conscious, defensive parents who are ready to leap up with a lawsuit at the first sign of trouble. This is not surprising, considering that many bullies come from families and homes that are aggressive too. Confrontation is simply a means to an end, the way the bully and his family get what they want out of life.

Faced with these roadblocks, it's understandable that schools seem a little slow off the mark in dealing with bullies. These legal and political hurdles have piled up over the years to form a steep, high mountain that must be scaled before we can unseat the bully from his perch up top.

CLASSROOM CRACKDOWN: DOES IT DO ANY GOOD?
Many schools have tried unseating the bully by instituting "Zero Tolerance" or "Get Tough" laws, policies that beef up the supervision and discipline in the schools coupled with tighter security measures, surveillance cameras, metal detectors, walkie-talkies and stiffer penalties for students involved in violence.

Many schools have started a "SchoolWatch" program. It began in a Miami-area school after a 12-year-old girl was raped. Based on the successful Neighborhood Watch program, schools post special warning signs, encourage the entire community to watch for trouble and focus on cooperation between students, staff and police to create a safe environment. In some schools, students are even eligible for a $1,500 reward if they turn in a violent school mate.

Another approach is to reexamine the lay-out of school buildings. Architects must now consider safety a high priority, incorporating fewer entrances through which unwelcome visitors can slip and a wide-open front hall-way in full view of the office. Even older-style schools are placing mirrors in strategic spots so that front-office staff can see what's going on in hidden corners and who is entering the school at all times.

However, some experts believe that relying on these measures, which are aimed primarily at the high-school level where fear for safety is most intense, is like relying on Band-Aids to cure a gaping wound. The practice, for example, of schools laying minor assault charges when-ever possible, is expensive and not terribly effective. Toronto criminologist Anthony Doob breaks it down to dollars and cents. If a youth does go into custody (and chances are slim if he's a first-timer), he will likely get 30 to 60 days, cost taxpayers $6,000 to $12,000, and come out worse than before. Alternatively, taxpayers could pay about $1,000 per child for an intensive intervention program aimed at aggressive children in kindergarten, which, unlike a prison sentence, offers proven results. "The problem is, it's easier for a politician to say he built more jails," Doob points out. "Nobody's afraid of kinder-garten kids."

There is no quick fix for violence, experts agree. They warn that if battling bullying isn't made a priority in the early grades, then the problem will only be worse for the next generation. And it won't be long until all North American schools are like a number of the shell-shocked ones in some big American cities, in which students line up to enter barbed-wire enclosed schools, one child at a time, face metal detectors, body- and bag-searches and cameras made from the high-tech space shuttle material, where they are forced to use ID cards to identify which wings of the school they are allowed to enter, with shot-gun-toting cops and dogs patrolling the halls and, in some cases, 16 police officers assigned to one hallway alone. And even then, such precautions may not work. The complicated conspiracy to bomb the Littleton high school in 1999 was carried out despite the presence of cameras and a security officer.

Granted, some technological solutions may be helpful. Walkie-talkies, for example, allow a teacher to go outside in the school yard and make direct contact with students. But cameras, metal detectors, bars on doors and windows convey the message that the school is unsafe, that teach-ers don't trust young people and that the adults are having trouble controlling them. Rather than diminishing the problem it may exacerbate it, creating an atmosphere that seethes with suspicion. And, as Toronto educator Gerard Cleveland warns, if you kick the bad kids out the school's front door, they'll walk right in through the back. Even if the aggressive kids are locked out, they will still hang around the park across the street, doing their dirty deeds there.

Unfortunately, today's climate of fear has produced a "boot camp" mentality—a politically driven get-tough approach that could one day turn every school into a fortress.

You don't need to look to the future to realize some-thing's wrong; just look to the past. Schools have been suspending children for years and nothing has changed. In the past, when bullying surfaced in a school, the offender would be carted off to the office for a slap on the wrist, maybe a suspension (which, to the bully, was like a mini mid-term vacation, a great chance to watch the soaps and *Oprah* and hang out with friends at noon) and the victim would be left on her own. That didn't work. Neither did counselling the students on their social skills. Counselling a bully in isolation doesn't work when she continues to be in such a highly reinforcing situation: every time she does it, she gets more money, power, popularity or prestige. When you get so many rewards from bullying, why would you want to stop?

What *has* been shown to work is the "whole-school" approach to stopping bullying and early, concerted intervention changing, not so much the building structure as the environmental structure. The extent of the problem today, especially among older students whose bullying is more organized, is such that it can't be handled by one part of the team alone. Police, parents, schools, community and students working together offer the only real chance for success.

And it's got to start early. Unfortunately, the "lighter" form of bullying among the very young tends to be ignored or trivialized until it's really serious, and by then it's more difficult to change. But by stopping it at the elementary level—before we let the bully out of the barn, so to speak—there is hope he won't grow to be such a big problem at high school.

THE "WHOLE-SCHOOL" SOLUTION

> *Tom, a family therapist in eastern Ontario, recalls listening to the heart-wrenching sobs of an 11-year-old client in his office practice. Jill told him about her living hell, days of taunting and teasing by the class bullies and threats of retribution*

should she ever tell. Her principal offered to hold
a once-a-year assembly to try to deal with the
bullying problem, an idea that astounded Tom.
"We wouldn't teach math once a year," he says.

So far no one has come up with any one program that
eliminates school bullying. There are programs that make
kids nicer, there are programs that make schools more
secure or reduce violent incidents, but there is no simple
cure, no magic bullet to wipe out the problem altogether.
Many schools, for example, have tried universal programs
designed to teach pro-social skills to all students. They
may prevent problems among "normal" children, but
studies show they don't help kids who have already been
identified as overly aggressive. Placing these aggressive
kids in special behavior classes is not enough, either.[7]

A battle is best won with a united front. The battle
against the bully is no exception. All components that
affect a child's life—her family and friends, the teachers,
principal and the neighborhood around her—must be
united against bullying in any form. And everyone in that
child's world must agree to do something about it. Children and adults alike need to change attitudes, to admit
that bullying does happen, to agree that it is a bad thing
and that it is not going to happen any more. That may be
one of the biggest challenges: convincing grownups that
there is a problem and opening their eyes and ears
enough to show them where it occurs and why.

As one police officer said, "If the same thing happened
to us, whether it was being assaulted or having something
stolen, we would call 911." Unfortunately, children are
expected to accept such bullying as part of growing up.
Those attitudes need to change.

Many studies have found that it can work. Bullying is less pronounced in schools where peaceful classrooms are a top priority. These are schools where teachers are knowledgeable about bullying problems, take them seriously, attach importance to the control and prevention of bullying and have a high number of teachers supervising the playground at recess.

> *Brenda grew to hate Tuesdays. That was the day her nine-year-old son, Robbie, would regularly return from school covered with bumps and scrapes. The kids called it "Bruise Day Tuesday" after their favorite heroes from the WWF. When one of the kids "power-slammed" Robbie—jumped on him with his full body weight—Brenda took him to hospital and pulled him out of the school. The principal called it "play fighting." With one adult supervising the playground for every 100 students, he insists his school is safe and even talked with the junior and senior grade students about the dangers of rough-housing and bullying. "You can't legislate good manners and good behavior," he shrugged.*

Making peace a priority does not mean setting aside a few minutes in health class or a school assembly to discuss aggression; nor does it mean wielding an iron hand on discipline problems. A better approach involves weaving lessons on aggression and conflict throughout the curriculum, including sexism and racism, impulse control, cooperation, peer counseling and anger management. If there is more talk about power-differential problems of all kinds then students may be more attuned to the abuse of power in the playground.

It can even help when teachers re-evaluate the way they maintain discipline in their own classrooms, substituting the traditional what-I-say-goes approach that capitalizes on power imbalance with a more democratic, shared ownership approach. When you enlist students' help in putting together a whole-school anti-bullying campaign, your chances of success are multiplied because they gain a sense of ownership and responsibility for making it work. Students can help spell out the consequences for bullying. One class may decide the bully gets no time on the computer, for example; another may opt for exclusion from a group activity. Bullies may be more influenced by rules their peers have made. They may also be more influenced when their peers have had a hand in resolving disputes, which is why peer mediation can be so successful with bullying problems. We will discuss this approach later in the chapter.

And when parents and the community join in the clean-up operation, there is a good chance bullying can be wiped out. The same community-wide approach has helped change attitudes about smoking, racism and drunk driving. Many believe it could work for bullying as well. It's called the "whole-school solution," and ideally includes a slew of wellness-based tactics, everything from breakfast programs to free extra-curricular activities, peer mentoring, non-competitive sports, cooperative learning and special celebrations to boost school spirit. On its own, no one program will solve the problem: some have immediate impact, others are more long-term. But combined with community consensus and commitment, together they may banish the schoolyard bully.

According to Yvonne Racine, research coordinator with the Centre for Studies of Children at Risk in Hamilton,

Ontario, many successful school-based programs have three important components: parent education (helping them deal with their kids consistently), social-skills training in the classroom and academic enrichment addressing a "horrible double whammy"—the tendency of kids who are behind in their schoolwork starting to misbehave, and kids who misbehave beginning to fall behind in their schoolwork. Experts suggest schools could tackle the problem from many directions:

- Medication or special support services could help children with speech and language impediments, learning disabilities, attention deficits or hyperactivity that may contribute to aggression.
- As a long-term preventative, high school students could be offered child-rearing classes and schools could be opened up to the community to provide drop-in centers or parent relief programs.
- After-school programs could offer kids an opportunity to build better friendships and take up hobbies.
- Schools could establish regular contact between the teacher, guidance counselor and principal and the families of high-risk children.[8]

One of the individuals who has had the most success in treating the bully problem is Dr. Dan Olweus. His country launched a nation-wide bully reduction program in 1983. By approaching the problem at three levels—the school, home and individual—Olweus says they reduced the amount of bullying by more than 50 per cent. His extensive research, carried out on a large scale over several years, is the only program to have clearly evaluated its success. He says he also found theft, vandalism and truancy declined, while students' satisfaction with school increased.

Olweus' approach has several components:

- School and staff were educated about the problem.
- Information and advice booklets were made available to parents.
- An inexpensive video about bullying was offered to the public.
- A classroom questionnaire helped draw a clear picture of how much bullying was taking place.

Olweus found that for best results the school (and ideally the home) should show warmth, positive interest and involvement, should closely monitor children's activities and should establish firm limits to unacceptable behavior. Non-hostile, non-physical punishment should be used. Students must be given generous praise when they follow the clearly defined bullying rules: not to bully others, to help students who are bullied and to include students who become easily left out.

Some experts believe that Olweus' success proves that half the bullies would not be bullies if their anonymity were removed. Many of these bullies may not be hardcore, incorrigible aggressors but simply kids who find bullying fun because they can get away with it. If they are told that bullying is a horrible thing, that they will be watched and that there are consequences to bullying, and if the rest of the student body reinforces that message, a lot of bullies may simply stop.

Before a school implements a whole-school anti-bullying policy (which is, incidentally, distinct from a regular behavior code, although such a code can reinforce the anti-bully policy), there should be in-depth discussions about what bullying is and where it's happening. A good place to start is with a school-wide confidential questionnaire. Begin with a definition of bullying (including all the subtle and covert forms) with several examples. The questionnaire should determine how often bullying happens, when and where. Young children could mark on a map where they feel unsafe. It should also ask how bullying is currently handled at school, and seek suggestions from students, staff and parents for making improvements. For more information on obtaining or conducting questionnaires, contact your school board psychologist.

The survey results could then be shared with staff, parents and students, and a working group formed to brainstorm solutions, using students' suggestions wherever possible. Decide whom parents should talk to if their child is being bullied, how the trouble spots can be better supervised, and what school procedures will be for dealing with bullying. There should be guidelines for investigating incidents and for responding positively and confidentially to victims who report. Timelines for action, regular meetings and communication with the school community will keep the commitment strong and the policy focused. Bullying could be discussed at staff meetings, with home and school groups, school councils and in the classroom; better yet, schools could hold regular meetings with representatives from all groups to discuss progress. At the beginning of each school year the anti-bully message should be sent out in order to cement the school's reputation as a bully-free zone.

In summary, the "whole-school" approach works when

- everyone—students, school staff, parents and community—agrees that bullying must stop;

- school staff, students and parents receive education and training to handle anger and conflict and on how to detect bullying and to support victims;
- students are closely supervised;
- positive reinforcement is used for non-bullying behavior;
- rules and consequences for bullying behavior are clearly spelled out.

WHAT THE SCHOOL CAN DO ON AN IMMEDIATE BASIS

- Students should be made aware that, when they are bothered by a bully, they should tell a trusted teacher, guidance counsellor, secretary or custodian. The entire school staff should be trained to respond properly and be committed to following through.

- Teachers who become aware of bullying can regroup students to change their social circles within the classroom and fragment any overly aggressive cliques.

- The bully's or victim's help can be enlisted in overseeing classroom tasks such as organizing recycling programs, for example, to help foster self-esteem and redirect their attention.

- Children who watch a bully incident and do nothing to help should be made aware that what they have done was wrong, that by not helping they are hurting. Schools should develop reasonable consequences to teach silent witnesses that they should be speaking out. The lesson should be taught that witnesses ought to walk away (depriving the bully of his audience), and speak out or tell an adult.

TEACHING THE ART OF MEDIATION

Peacemaking programs have been another highly successful way to put a damper on bullies in elementary and junior high schools. This approach is often called Reconciliation, the fourth R to be added to the teacher's list. In a

THE "WHOLE-SCHOOL" APPROACH: MORE IDEAS

Other schools have hit upon a variety of successful approaches to quell bullying. When combined with other programs and applied throughout the school, the anti-bully message is sure to get across.

- In one school a boy with a disability was getting the brunt of the bullying. Teachers paired him up with a conscientious student to keep an eye on him, act as his ambassador and inform teachers if any more bullying occurred.

- In another school students who are bullied are encouraged to write the bully a letter describing what happened and how it made them feel. They say in the letter that if the bullying stops, no discipline will be taken. Teachers say the method has proven successful in many cases.

- In many schools, children are taught as early as kindergarten how to resist peer pressure, not only to bolster them for the bully battles to come but also to help them say no to other negative influences such as drugs, sex and smoking.

- Some teachers' groups and government departments are trying pull the problem out by the roots by helping communities organize and address underlying causes such as drugs and family violence.

- Teachers find that when students are on the rotary system, switching classrooms every 40 minutes as they do in junior high and middle schools, bullies have a field day. They can jab an elbow in here, a shoulder in there, or casually and inconspicuously dump someone's books and not be noticed in the crammed between-class mayhem. Several schools have tried changing class schedules to see if less traffic in the halls cuts down bullying there.

- One school found it helped to give students an extra-long break between classes in the afternoon to let them blow off steam in the school yard, rather than in the crowded between-class hallways.

- In some schools "bully courts" have been held with some success. The judges were students elected by their peers who heard complaints of bullying brought to them by other children. The judges set the punishments, such as apologizing, doing pages of arithmetic, cleaning or doing something nice for the victim. Teachers found the bullies who were "tried" in this manner were more open to criticism from peers, and the process helped all children understand the need for rules. Dr. Dan Olweus, however, throws in a word of caution: bullies are good at talking themselves out of trouble and they may do so while the timid, intimidated victims keep mum.

- Some schools have invited social workers, psychologists or counsellors to run small group meetings to talk about bullying with the children. Students then write about their feelings and make anti-bullying posters, poems or plays to share with the school.
- To battle bullying on the bus, schools could work with school-bus lines to encourage more consistency among drivers (frequent staff turnover can lead to inconsistent discipline).
- Victim support groups and assertiveness training programs have been helpful at some schools to show victims how to stand up for themselves.
- A special mailbox, placed in an inconspicuous spot in the school, can offer fearful kids a place to voice their concerns anonymously.

nutshell, it involves children helping children to solve their own disputes. Students are selected by either teachers or other students to be peacemakers (also known as conflict managers or mediators). In an intensive training program they learn to defuse disputes and help classmates work out peaceful resolutions. Then, in teams of two, wearing special identifying hats, crests, or T-shirts, they patrol the playground, buses and hallways looking for trouble.

The reason peacemaking programs work is because they approach bullying at ground level. In most bullying episodes, other children are involved one way or another, whether watching the action, trying to stop it or landing a few punches of their own. But the few times that children try to intervene, only about half the time are their interventions appropriate. The rest of the time they haven't a clue; quite often the would-be rescuers end up bullying the bully instead or getting hurt themselves. Lessons in conflict resolution can show kids the way, teaching skills that for a long time we thought were innate: how to communicate, mediate, deal with aggression and solve problems. Children are involved anyway; we might as well make use of them. And experience proves their participation can be highly effective.

After only a few years, the program has become extremely popular. Today, most local school boards across North America are trying mediation programs and reporting some success. Teachers say that training kids to be negotiators, able to sort out fights and smooth childhood's turbulent waters, has reduced the level of violence and aggression in their schools. They see fewer fights, less verbal abuse and more caring behavior among students.

The program works this way: two peacemakers come upon a conflict in the school yard. Often, because they are students and can blend in with the others, the peacemakers detect bullying that would normally be hidden from a teacher's view. First, the peacemakers make sure that both students are willing to solve their problem with the mediators' help, rather than a teacher's. (There is, of course, great incentive to handle it on their own rather than face a grownup.) The students must agree on the ground rules: to tell the truth, to behave respectfully without name-calling, to listen without interrupting and to be willing to carry out the terms of the final agreement.

They then go to a quiet area and each tells the peacemakers what happened, how it made them feel and how he or she believes it could have been prevented. This storytelling time is important because it gives hot emotions time to cool off. The peacemakers sum up what has been said to ensure it is all understood. Together the students think of solutions. The peacemakers write down all the ideas, far-fetched or otherwise, then read them back to the participants to determine the favored one.

The students then agree where, when and how the solution will be carried out and shake hands. Sometimes they sign a contract agreeing to the terms of the solution. Everything is logged in the teacher or guidance counsellor's record book.

In some areas, the peacemaking program coincides with workshops on aggression, role-playing and classroom discussions about anger. Teachers are taught to incorporate the approach in the classroom, watching for "teachable moments." When conflict arises in the classroom, they encourage the students to figure out how to deal with it on the spot. They may even incorporate a discussion on cooperation in math class or learn how a body processes anger in science class.

When students are involved in choosing who will be peacemakers, they usually pick the popular children or the bullies, because they are seen as strong people. Some teachers find this is an ideal way to capitalize on the bully's natural leadership abilities, although some of the bullies-turned-peacemakers have trouble with the role, with the teasing they may get and with learning to be creative with words. Generally, however, teachers say the bullies like being powerful and this is a way for them to get power without getting into trouble. They learn the difference between dominating and leading.

The main benefit of this program is that it teaches children there are other ways to respond to conflict besides aggression or passivity, it gives them the tools to do it and it lets them practice those techniques in their own relationships. They also learn to be good listeners and to disassociate emotions from issues.

But while mediation can work with the more obvious conflicts, it doesn't always work in serious cases of bullying and aggression; students can't be expected to solve the high-level stuff on their own. Sometimes there is too marked a power differential; sometimes the victim is too helpless to truly benefit from a mediation process designed to take part between equals. And it often ignores the subtle stuff, the childhood underworld of cruel comments and subtle harassment that takes place unseen beneath the surface of a typical recess playground. Usually adult intervention and support are required.

THE PROBLEM WITH RECESS

The activity by the back fence appears to be your typical, garden-variety recess rough-housing. But look closely. Most of the boys are joking around, but the fellow in the middle is not. Gradually, their good-natured, exaggerated movements, common to harmless, rough-and-tumble play, become tight, tough and power-packed. If you really watch, you can see the pretend wrestling kick turn into the thud of a real, mean, intent-to-harm kick in the young boy's side. If you can get close enough, look at the victim's face. His expression tells all: he doesn't seem to be enjoying this at all. From a distance, however, their

*activity is unremarkable. The bullies get away
with it yet again.*

Teachers and peacemakers tend not to intervene in the
more subtle kind of bullying. Horseplay with malicious
undertones goes unnoticed. Social ostracism is out of
adults' sight and reach. Nor do adults notice the fleeting
kind of bullying that is surprisingly common: a quick,
cutting remark or a foot stuck out in front of someone as
she walks by. One study found that teachers intervened
in only 4 per cent of these bullying episodes. It wasn't
that they didn't care; they simply didn't know it was
happening.

This hidden harassment takes a well-trained eye and
lots of work with the entire school population to eradicate. And it calls for a fresh new look at our traditional
idea of recess activity.

*The boys began beating him casually, almost
routinely. The victim seems to have accepted his
role just as routinely. Soon you can hear the
thumps on his body. The boys carry on light
conversation as they beat him. One says, "Get
him with your knife." Another boy, holding something in his hand, says, "I'm going to take his
earlobe off." Someone else laughs. "Yeah, and
mail it to someone." More laughter.*

*The boy is on the ground, limply accepting a
kick in the leg, in the stomach, in the head. One
of the boys takes a running jump and lands on
him just like the body-crushing leaps of a big-time
wrestling hero. The victim tries searching for the
25 cents he says he lost in the dirt. He seems to be*

vainly struggling to retain some dignity, as if he is trying to show that the reason he's upset is because of his lost quarter—not because he is hurt. But the beating continues.

This is another scene from Debra Pepler's tapes, undeniably painful to watch. What do the boy's parents think when he comes home covered in bruises? Pepler wonders. And what is this brutalization doing to his self-esteem?

"What's striking about this," Pepler says, "is that this seems to be a common event for them at recess time."

Pepler says these studies have convinced her of the importance of vigilant monitoring of the school yard at recess. Many recess monitors are kindly volunteers or part-time help who have no experience or real training for what can be a very difficult task. The monitors often spend more time talking with each other or with the easy-to-get-along-with children, Pepler says, than in maintaining an eagle eye on the action.

Schools may be able to make great headway in battling bullying by providing more, and better-trained, playground monitoring. Adults on yard duty should be aware of the bullying hot spots, be able to detect subtle, covert bully problems and be trained to deal with them. Some of the conflict may be avoided simply by giving the kids more to do outside. How many schools have a faded old hopscotch patch on the sidewalk that nobody plays with because nobody knows how? It may help to teach kids what it's for, help them organize other outdoor games and structure a variety of activities at recess to get everyone equally involved. Pepler says one school discovered there was more friendly, mixed-gender play after a phys-ed teacher taught them some playground games.

TIPS TO HELP CHILDREN GET THROUGH RECESS IN A HEALTHIER WAY

- Increasing playground supervision can be one of the best approaches to school bullying, provided those supervisors are well-trained.
- Make sure that the school has a quality physical education program, one that not only teaches children games to play, but also teaches social skills, how to follow rules, and develops positive views of themselves and others. These are skills the children can then take with them into the playground. The instructor should be a qualified, well-trained and enthusiastic phys-ed teacher who knows how to teach children to accept others for the way they are.
- A teacher, preferably the gym teacher, can teach children games that can be transferred to the playground. These should be simple enough that they can organize themselves with minimal effort. Games that require smaller groups are more successful than those involving huge numbers of students.
- Schools should ensure there is plenty of equipment available to children at recess to discourage fighting over the use of too few resources. Each classroom could have its own games equipment box, with color-coded balls, etc. The home-room teacher can help children sign out equipment, which would include inexpensive items like skipping ropes and balls.
- Parents and teachers can get together to make and collect simple games and recess toys—for example, paint a handball court against a wall, sew beanbags and paint targets on the tarmac, make paddlebats out of plywood, make frisbees from paper plates, or collect discarded tennis balls from local tennis clubs.
- One school found that skipping rope sales made a great fundraiser. The school sold inexpensive skipping ropes to raise money. In the end, almost all of the students had their

own skipping rope and there were extras to be kept in the game box for the students who occasionally forget to bring theirs.

- Another school found it helpful to add more basketball hoops so that there was one for each grade.

- Games like Pogs, Crazy Bones and Pokemon collections—fads that have swept through schools like wild-fire in recent years—may be annoying to teachers when they interfere with classroom work. But when the play is well enough monitored that the younger students aren't taken advantage of, these games can teach kids valuable lessons in negotiating and conflict resolution while keeping them busy and out of trouble.

- Older students—those in Grades 6 to 8—can form a leadership club. Members volunteer as playground leaders and are trained to help younger children start group games, help manage equipment and referee.

- Games that work well at recess include a variety of tag games, relay races and hopscotch. For younger children (aged five to nine), good bets are jacks, marbles, clapping games, string games, ball games, Simon Says, leapfrog, Duck, Duck, Goose, Mother May I, and Red Light, Green Light. Older children are more challenged by games of strategy—King of the Hill, Capture the Flag, Tug-of-War, organized sports, card games and charades. Wherever possible there should be an emphasis on cooperative games in which children play together to achieve a goal, and students should be encouraged to join in at their own pace.

For more ideas, check the resource section at the end of this book.

When children are left to their own means, they can become antsy with boredom or untapped energy and can turn play into pain. Bullying is a crime of opportunity

and in many playgrounds, it seems, there is opportunity
to spare.

WORKING WITH THE POLICE

> *It's late in the school year, a few days before*
> *classes end for the summer, and someone has set*
> *a fire in an inner city school. Everyone is playing*
> *dumb and the principal is stymied. In the gym,*
> *Officer Mark McKeon tries his hand at it. "You*
> *know what," he says, in his casual, street-savvy*
> *style, "a couple of you guys did a really silly thing*
> *last night. I don't want to have to spend days*
> *trying to sort this out. It's time for one or two of*
> *you to have a private talk in the office." When he*
> *leaves, he asks the principal to phone him if they*
> *find the culprits. Ten minutes later he gets the*
> *call. Two students, in front of everyone, stood up*
> *and fessed up. "You guys showed real guts,"*
> *McKeon told them later. "You're not in any trou-*
> *ble. Go get ready for your graduation party."*

McKeon thinks he knows why the troublemakers decided
to take the rap. The Toronto police officer has spent three
years getting to know the school, and it is working.
McKeon coaches them, works on their drama productions, and teaches a highly effective lecture series on
Youth and the Law that throws a whole new light on
bullying. First, he asks the students—who have reached
the age when they can be charged in Canada—what kids
do to break the law. He writes the words "harassment,"
"threats" and "assault" on the blackboard. Then he
explores with them the difference between teasing (your

buddy missed the net in a soccer game and you rib him about it afterwords) and harassment (you continue to bug him about it for days); the difference between a simple bump in the hall and an assault offense; and what the name is for the person who does all these illegal things. When they realize it's the school bully, and that they can be charged for some of these misbehaviors, McKeon says, a lightbulb seems to switch on in their heads. They realize that they could be in very big trouble. And, because they have come to see police officers as human beings, this knowledge holds a lot more meaning for them.

For kids in the higher grades, police involvement can have a powerful effect. In the case of older children, bullying can often be a euphemism for what is, in fact, a crime, and what should, in fact, involve the police. If we were robbed, assaulted or intimidated, we would call the police. Why shouldn't we treat children just as seriously? But if police involvement is going to work, it's got to be handled sensitively. Parents and school administrators need to get together with the police without getting defensive. Quite often, police officers say, parents are defensive about their kids' behavior while administrators are defensive about the school's reputation. As a result, little gets accomplished.

Like Officer Mark McKeon, many schools and police forces have found it helps to lay the groundwork first so that, when an incident occurs, everyone is prepared. Several police forces have programs in which officers regularly visit schools, hoping to set up a relationship with the students and a presence in the school. Some even hold annual banquets with the students to better open the lines of communication. Setting up a Crime Watch program—similar in nature to the already established

Neighborhood Watch—has had a significant impact on crime rates in some schools. Another approach, called Tackle Violence and produced by the Metro Toronto police force, includes a video and police presentation that gives kids a gritty, realistic picture of what happens when kids gang up on each other. Many schools organize a cop-school match. One police officer is assigned to that school to act as a resource for students and teachers, educate children about the law, and teach them how to protect themselves if they are getting picked on. The police officer also attends dances and sports events and is always the officer who responds in incidents of violence. Administrators say that if a random selection of on-duty officers marches in and out of the school when violence erupts, there isn't the same kind of conscientious follow-through as there is when the police officer knows the students, the culture and the demographics of the school.

Other schools have stopped calling in uniformed police officers to deal with serious bullying problems. Their uniforms tend to broadcast their presence to the entire school and word gets out that anyone who tattles is in trouble. Immediately mouths seal shut. Instead these schools call upon the plainclothes officers in the street-crime unit, men and women who are trained in the subtleties of getting kids to talk and can instruct the school in the best methods of dealing with violence.

Most swarming incidents take place in areas where teens congregate away from school—shopping centers, theaters, tourist sights and sporting events. Police say one of their biggest problems is getting kids to report the swarming. That's because the victim is usually a "soft target": a student skipping out of school and hanging out where he isn't supposed to be or a young tourist visiting a big city who has slipped away from adult supervision. For victims who want to complain about bullying by gangs but fear retaliation, Metro Toronto police are offering new, powerful protection: victims who report bullying to police are given pager numbers for round-the-clock protection. There are also attempts to keep officers assigned to the same area for several years in order to build up some expertise and rapport in the neighborhood. Extensive conditions are now being imposed on kids who are out on bail or probation, including curfews and orders that the bully must go to class and must stay away from the group. The bully knows that if his gang attacks the victim again as retaliation for ratting, the bully will be locked up.

Another popular new program in the schools is Student Crime Stoppers. With the help of posters and school assemblies, students are made aware of a 24-hour "snitch line" that lets children report crimes—bullying, assaults, theft—to local police—anonymously. Administrators in schools where the program is in place report a considerable drop in criminal activity.

When police and school authorities handle a bullying incident with sensitivity, everyone—bully, victim and the student observers—gets a positive lesson. Not only do they learn that bullying will be punished and the victim will be supported, but they also learn that the police force is on their side.

DON'T FORGET THE VICTIM

It's one of those jarring, abrasive music videos that seem to get played on the music channel over and over again. It focuses on a young child, obviously teased and misunderstood by his classmates and teachers. Words of distress flash on the screen, along with cruel, laughing faces, and finally he breaks down. Then there is an image of the boy naked in the woods, the fires of damnation raging around him, his face alight with new-found power, and a final scene of destruction: a silent classroom strewn with students' bodies soaked in blood.

The video could be any victim's daydream, a fantasy he plays out in his mind when his tormentors just won't let up. It is, of course, an extreme version of the victim's anguish, but similar things have happened, the most deadly occurring in Littleton, Colorado, when 15 students and a teacher died. It was, unfortunately, not the first time neglected, troubled kids sought revenge with violence. It's the kind of crime that makes an occasional meteoric splash in the news: a victim whose suffering festers unnoticed until violence finally erupts. This is why it is so important that adults, in their eagerness to combat bullying, don't overlook the victim and his simmering pain.

When your self-esteem is already at rock bottom, you don't want to hear more negative messages: that it's partly your fault or that you should have told someone sooner. And most of all, you don't want to be ignored. You want respect. Quite often that is the last thing the victim receives.

"When this poor little kid gets knocked down, the teacher usually asks him if he's all right and then focuses all his attention on the bully," says one small-town vice-principal. "The little tyke on the ground gets forgotten and that reinforces the message that he isn't important."

To avoid that problem, school staff need to have a well-specified strategy for dealing with bullying incidents, one that takes into account the victim's needs as well. When teachers encounter a bullying situation in the playground, the victim should be attended to first. The bully can be dealt with later, preferably when there's no audience.

Mary believes that her son Alan was handled in a sensitive way. One morning she discovered her happy little seven-year-old clinging to his bed, hiding under the covers of the top bunk. He didn't want to go to school and his mom couldn't make him. After much questioning, she discovered one of the children had been calling him names. She finally persuaded him to accompany her to the vice-principal's office.

The vice-principal told Alan that the bullying was not his fault, nor was it his problem. It was the bully's problem and the school was going to do something about it. The school did, letting the bully know that this kind of behavior was not acceptable. But for Alan, and Mary, the most impressive part of this well-handled experience was the respect Alan was given. Several weeks later the vice-principal spoke to him in private again, making certain that no more bullying was happening and letting Alan know they hadn't forgotten him and they were taking the whole thing very seriously.

Schools should also be aware of the victim's very real fear of revenge. One mother remembers when her 12-year-old son Tony came home from school in tatters. She told the school what had happened and the next day the vice-principal called the bully into his office. "Tony tells me you've been beating him up," he said. Of course, Tony was beaten up again by the bully and his friends, out for revenge. But he never told his mom again. He made that mistake the first time. "He used to come home all bruised," Jan says, "his jacket ripped up, and tell me he fell down the ravine."

It could have been handled better. If the vice-principal had taken the time to make some subtle inquiries he might have discovered that other children were being harassed by this bully. Even if other kids weren't involved, he could still have confronted the bully without naming names and thus preserved the victim's anonymity.

Child psychologists worry about these neglected victims. When schools make referrals for psychological help it is usually for those who are aggressive or hyperactive. But at least half the disorders in the schools are internalized, says Dr. Kenneth Rubin, professor of psychology at the University of Waterloo, Ontario. By the age of 11 or 12, these internalizers are the ones most likely to cry out for help. The loud, aggressive children tend to get the attention, since their behavior disrupts the entire class. But the kids who feel poorly about themselves, who may be more lonely and depressed, are the ones who have to ask for help. Educators should be trained to identify the quiet children who are suffering in silence and get them the help they need before it's too late. According to the National Association of School Psychologists, childhood victims display many characteristics of post-traumatic stress disorder, including blocked learning and symptoms of serious emotional problems. The association says schools should offer counseling and recovery programs for victims of school violence.

TIPS FOR IDENTIFYING THE HIDDEN VICTIM

He or she
- seems generally unhappy;
- at recess seems isolated or wanders from group to group without really belonging to any of them;
- hesitates to come to school;
- is distracted; is unable to concentrate or attend to the task at hand;
- is reluctant to go outside at recess, hides in the washroom or library or hovers near the teacher or walls;
- may often be the one pushed out of line or involved in unbalanced fights;
- is usually the last one chosen for teams;
- seems to "whine" a lot about mistreatment or negative incidents.

It would be easier to identify the child who is suffering if teachers made it known that they were available and took bullying seriously. The victim would therefore be more likely to step forward and ask for help.

MORE PEACE TACTICS
- Some experts call for a strict protocol for all youth-service providers (principals, teachers, youth counsellors) so that there is a mandatory course of action when bullying erupts, the way there is for reports of sexual assault. Principals should be required to call police, parents, child-welfare workers or any other agency when it's deemed appropriate.
- Teachers should question their own behavior; they themselves may be bullying students without realizing it. They should ask: "Am I bullying the kids in

my class? Should I be listening more, opening up the discussions more?"

- Find positive role models for shy or anxious children. One teacher tells of a small girl from Rumania with a very poor self-image, thanks to bullying by other children. Dark-skinned and sallow-faced, she didn't look like any of the other kids and they teased her incessantly until she finally holed herself up in the library at recess and noon. The librarian says she learned that a student teacher who was beautiful and self-confident was also Rumanian. She asked the woman to speak with the girl about their shared heritage, to let her know she could be proud of being Rumanian. Today this girl feels much better about herself and has a group of friends who are reliable and kind.

- There should be a systemic approach to tattling. Teachers at recess are constantly bombarded with complaining kids. Sometimes it's nothing—just a minor squabble—and sometimes it's serious—the fourth teacher that child has complained to about bullying and all of them have dismissed the complaints. Adults and children alike need to adopt the attitude that it's courageous and correct to speak out against injustice.

- Students need to be encouraged to persist if their complaint is not taken seriously, and teachers may need to be reminded to keep their ears open for real trouble. Bullies are very good at not getting caught, and threats and intimidation are especially easy to hide from adult view. Sometimes a bully's antics are so subtle they can be done right under the teacher's nose. One gym teacher recounts how bullies were forcing the weaker children to stay on the bench and out of the basketball game when the match was close. The teacher was sitting right there among the students but didn't know what was going on until later.

- Parents who are concerned about bullying may want to suggest to their child's teacher that he plan a lesson on tolerance, personal differences or anger management. They may also want to discuss the possibility that lessons in psychology be taught in high schools or even earlier, to give children insight into issues of fear, power and self-esteem or a very basic law course for elementary school children so they will recognize when their rights are being trampled by the bully.

- Parents may also want to organize a group of volunteers who arrange activities for recess, so boredom doesn't lead to bullying.

- Because so much of the whole-school solution relies on community commitment, it's important that everyone is kept informed. When a new pro-social program is implemented in a school, it should be introduced and explained to students and parents with the help of meetings or school newsletters. This way everyone is involved and lessons can be reinforced and evaluated at home.

- Create a suggestion box for students to offer ideas about making their school safe. Schools should acknowledge and respond to ideas so kids know they are being heard.

PROGRAMS THAT MAKE A DIFFERENCE
Peace By Peace

They share the same passion for designer labels and

baggy pants, watch the same movies, listen to the same music, laugh at the same jokes. The children, and "teachers," in the Peace by Peace program have a lot in common. And that may be why this new approach to an old problem works.

In New Haven, Connecticut, Harlem, New York and Toronto, Canada, educators have discovered the value of "cool," and they are using it to wipe out the schoolyard bully. Peace by Peace links university students with those in Grades 4, 5 and 6 to explore more peaceful approaches to play. For 10 weeks, the older students—all volunteers—spend one and a half hours talking and playing cooperative games with their younger charges. They teach them about conflict de-escalation, body language, self-esteem, anger management and cool-off techniques. They discuss "inner power" and how to use it to beat the bully. They learn how to play games that rely on teamwork, where no one loses, no one is excluded and everyone wins. They bring those new approaches to the playground. Then on the 11th week everyone involved in the program gets together for a huge peace festival, a very concrete way to see what a peaceful community can look like.

"There's just something special about 20-year-olds teaching 10-year-olds," says Robin Sacks, founder and director of the program that links the University of Toronto with the Toronto District School Board. "We tell them we know it's tough to be 10, but this is what we did when we were 10," says Sacks. "It's a role-modeling relationship. We can tell them that this is what's cool and they respect that."

Roots of Empathy

He was just 13, but he oozed attitude. His head was

shaved. He was covered in tattoos. And when he was younger, he had watched his father murder his mom. "Johnny" was one rough customer.

But one school day, some softness slipped through.

The Roots of Empathy class was finishing up and students were moving back to their desks. The parent who had visited Johnny's classroom as part of the class was packing up to leave. Johnny saw the baby's Snugli and asked, casually, how it worked. Just as casually, he tried it on. Then, gingerly, he lifted the baby, quietly, close to his chest. He took the baby to a corner and sat down. Then he rocked. Just rocked. And his teachers stood in silent awe.

Sometimes the biggest miracles come in the smallest packages. In this Toronto classroom, it was a baby who taught a child about emotions.

Developed by former kindergarten teacher Mary Gordon, Roots of Empathy is capturing interest around the world for the way it takes a very simple concept—the unbridled love of a parent for his child—and uses it to teach children empathy.

And when empathy increases, aggression decreases.

The key to this program is the classes' "adoption" of a baby. Once a month the baby and his parent (often the father) visit the classroom to teach the youngsters about "baby talk"—the non-verbal cues infants use to express emotion. Students then explore their own and others' emotions and how to respond to them sensitively. They make peek-a-boo books and write poetry for the baby, analyze sleep patterns, calculate the cost of cloth diapers and discover that babies—and all people—can speak without words.

Students watch the baby cry and see what the father

does. They're then asked to think about their own lives, about how they can tell, for example, if their friend is upset and what they can do to help. Mary Gordon, currently administrator of parenting programs with the Toronto school board, says the program has flourished and is now being adopted by the Canadian Institute of Child Health for implementation across country, and is moving into Japan, Scotland and England and the United States. Because babies wear their emotions on their drool-stained sleeves, the older kids learn to deal with feelings in a less self-conscious way, Gordon explains, and they discover how to put themselves in someone else's shoes—a valuable skill in the battle against bullying.

Acting Out about Acting Out

Annie listened to the voices on the cassette tape and cringed. She could hear the kids in her class making fun of her body, calling her a monkey, saying that she had no breasts and looked like a boy. She switched off the tape recorder, went into her grandmother's medicine cabinet, and popped 20 pills.

Fortunately, Annie survived the suicide attempt and today she draws upon that experience to help other victims of bullying. Like many other high school students across North America, she is using her drama class to reach out to children and teach about violence and bullying. In Annie's program, a theater cooperative in a Toronto-area school, older students perform for younger students, hold workshops, debates and discussions on empathy and schoolyard bullying. They also provide the elementary school teachers with an information package and offer to keep in touch with students who want to chat.

Experts say drama is an excellent forum for addressing bullying and other sensitive issues like eating disorders and sexuality. Children's literature can offer the same benefits. Both allow children to see, and experience vicariously, the role power plays in human relationships and how many alternatives there are to solving a problem. It also lets them have thoughtful discussions about what can be an embarrassing subject. Like the popular children's books that let kids choose a solution then turn to the corresponding page to see the outcome, literature and drama can help children think "outside the box."

Campaigning in the Streets

It started with a group of mothers in Richmond, Washington, who were fed up with the violence that was poisoning their children's lives. They banded together to form Mothers Against Violence in America and took their message to the streets, to policy makers and members of the community. Teenagers in the United States took up the crusade, forming school-based groups called Students Against Violence Everywhere. They brought the campaign into their schools to promote non-violent ways to handle conflict, staging violence-free Teen Nights, anti-violence poster contests, forums and country-wide anti-violence conferences. A similar crusade spread north to Canada where the "LOVE" Campaign began. Let's Oppose Violence Everywhere, formed by the 700,000-strong Ontario Secondary School Students' Association, is encouraging youth to sign a pledge to refrain from using violence in their lives. Pledgers wear blue ribbons and are offered seminars on how to lobby for peer-helping courses and continue the grassroots fight for peace.

The Mentor Method

Our children are adrift, warns American poet Robert Bly. In his book *The Sibling Society*, he says we have abandoned our kids to the "devouring giants" of television, consumerism and spiritual impoverishment, and have stolen from them the authority figures they need to look up to.

If this is true, we've created a great breeding ground for bullies. In the absence of positive leadership, children drift toward negative leaders like bullies—but proponents of mentoring think they can fill the gap. Across the continent this old-fashioned, one-on-one relationship is gaining new fans as kids discover that grown-ups may have something to offer after all. In fact, studies show that this kind of significant friendship can save an at-risk child from a life of trouble.

In many of the new mentorships, adults offer young people their time and wisdom. There are athletic-based mentors, in which university athletes link up with high school athletes who in turn mentor elementary students. There are informal mentorships offered through family service agencies and a variety of screening organizations. And there is the new Big Brother In-School Mentoring Program which began in the U.S. in the early 1990s and is now increasingly popular in Canada. Mentors, often a senior living nearby or an employee who can slip away at lunch or who has been given the time off, spend one hour a week with a child at his school. What they do together varies: they may work on the computer, do homework, play in the gym. Most importantly, they are there to listen and provide hope. (For more information, check the Resources section.)

Another approach is being tried in Toronto. In the

Mentoring and School Co-op Program, students who have been having trouble at school are paired with a mentor (who is ideally of the same racial or ethnic background) and are also given a co-op work placement. It is hoped that the mentor will offer emotional support and the co-op provide a relevance that the regular school could not.

A child entering a new school can be a prime target for bullies. To allay that concern, some schools arrange mentors for new students. At some high schools, older students are assigned to accompany younger students during the first few weeks.

Other schools have brought in Prime Mentors of Canada, an award-winning program designed to tap the potential of at-risk creative children in Grades 4 through 8. Children are matched with an adult based on their shared interests. During a 12-to-18 week period, the pair chooses and creates a project which the child then presents to the class. By focusing on a child's strengths, this program boosts her self-esteem along with her social skills. (For more information, see the Resources Section.)

Effective Behavior Support

It's another school assembly honoring the students of the month at a suburban elementary school. The list of honorees is a long one and the pint-sized audience sitting on the gymnasium floor is increasingly restless. One after another the students are called to the front to receive the certificate. There are 75 names on the list this morning. Kids on the floor poke each other's backsides, snicker, whisper and get an occasional dirty look from a teacher. When her name is called, seven-year-old Emma walks shyly to the front to accept the piece of paper. She doesn't have a clue what it's for. Emma is inclined to believe her older brother (one of the few in the school who has not received the award) who insists it's just a name pulled from a hat. At the end of the day, the award is crumpled into the bottom of her backpack along with a myriad of other papers, and forgotten.

Awards for good behavior can be highly effective. They can also be highly useless if they're not handled properly and done in conjunction with other school-wide behavior programs. There are so many good, and not so good, ideas on school discipline today that many schools may be overwhelmed, lose steam, or take the wrong approach. New Westminster Secondary School has found a way to make it work: At the Vancouver-area school, students spotted doing a good dead get a B.A.D. slip—short for Big Awesome Doings. Students who receive the coveted awards get lots of praise and, if their slip is pulled in a monthly draw, a $20 CD gift certificate. Along with the B.A.D. slips, the school has implemented a more streamlined system to deal with students who misbehave. Seventeen other schools in the Vancouver area are trying the same approach, and in the first year there has been a noticeable drop in discipline problems.

It's part of a new program called Effective Behavior Support (EBS) based at the University of Oregon. Oregon, and four other U.S. universities, joined to form the Center on Positive Behavioral Interventions and Supports, funded by U.S. Department of Education. Its goal is to spread the word about what disciplinary practices have been *proven* to work and help schools with implementation.

EBS gives schools like New Westminster the decision-making structure to help them wade through the options, then keep them focused. A leadership team is formed that includes parents to find out which programs would best fit their school and then get the whole school moving in the same direction. Schools that have used the EBS program report that the number of office discipline referrals decreased between 20 and 60 per cent over the first year.

Safe and Caring Schools Project

It's a hot and lazy Friday afternoon, and the last class of the day for the Grade 12 students at a high school in Alberta. History class. World War II. The clock ticks loudly. Somebody yawns. One or two slouch deep in their desks, nodding off with boredom. Suddenly, the class snaps awake again. What's that the teacher said? We may have something in common with Hitler and Mussolini? Gangs in Alberta, mass mentality in Europe? All at once the class is abuzz as the teacher opens up the floor to a discussion on gang mentality, the way peers influence behavior and how individual choice influences everyday life. The bell rings. Not a soul gets up to leave.

It's a dramatic example of how effective it can be to incorporate social skills lessons in the school curriculum. And it's part of new efforts to make schools in Alberta safer. The Safe and Caring Schools Project is a comprehensive violence-prevention undertaking designed to encourage socially responsible and respectful behavior. Begun in April 1996 with a grant from the provincial Minister of Education, the project begins with an assessment of each school to identify its strengths and weaknesses. The schools then have access to a list of resources, manuals and videos describing strategies that work, including a community program for adults and older teens designed to help them model and reinforce positive social behavior.

A Uniform Solution

Every morning of every school day, a fight is going on somewhere between parents and their kids over what to wear. Should it be a trendy Tommy top and platform sneakers, or the more conservative button-down and sensible shoes? This expensive hat, or that cheaper no-name one? Don't be mistaken; this is serious stuff for young people today. At many schools, what you wear can make or break your reputation. It's so competitive that some groups of bullies who covet the designer look are mobbing and robbing for clothes.

Not so in Long Beach, California. In 1994 the Long Beach Board of Education voted to become the country's first public school district to require uniforms. Today, 64,000 elementary and middle-school students must wear a shirt and bottoms in a color that has been chosen by their school.

The award-winning program has shown astounding results; within four years, crime in elementary and middle schools dropped 90 per cent. President Bill Clinton praised the program, saying, "When one student is no longer obsessed by another student's sneakers or designer jackets...crime and violence go down, attendance and learning go up." Other schools across the continent are now experimenting with similar dress codes and interest is growing around the world.

Educators in Long Beach say the uniform idea works best when there is a high level of parental support, when each school can select its own uniforms, when there is assistance arranged for disadvantaged children, and when the results are monitored and communicated to the community.

Some observers worry that the uniforms will stamp out

students' individuality, but those who have tried it say it teaches students that individuality is on the inside. John Chapman, principal of Quinte Secondary School in Belleville, says bullies used to swipe students' baseball caps and then threatened victims not to tell. Parents just assumed the expensive hats were lost. That doesn't happen now that the school's dress code—including a no-hat rule—is in effect. Chapman says the individuality concern is a non-issue. "There are other ways of expressing your individuality," he says, "like with good decisions or standing on your own feet or not getting sucked into peer group problems."

Gardening for Peace

In a tiny plot of paradise surrounded by trees and flowers, three six-year-old girls are sharing their school's "Friendship Bench," singing to a statue of St. Francis of Assisi as the birds scratch in the ground nearby. It is a sight that warms the heart of Julia Morton-Marr.

Morton-Marr, along with Eric Foster, founded International School Peace Gardens in 1994 to develop peace-building educational programs. The three girls at the Ontario Catholic school were benefiting from the program that encourages schools to design and grow a garden as a symbol of peace.

A growing number of schools have discovered that Nature can bring out the nurture in children. Child-centered gardens are sprucing up schools and bringing peace to playgrounds all over the world. School gardens can be cross-curricular and cross-generational. Students may build benches in shop class, or scarecrows in art. They may be high school science students helping elementary school children garden, or seniors and youngsters sharing a schoolyard plot. Whatever form they take, school gardens build social skills, responsibility, pride, cooperation, patience and community spirit. And when there is something nice to look at that makes them proud, children may be more inclined to pick on weeds instead of each other.

Morton-Marr, whose Peace Gardens concept has spread world-wide from Ghana to Slovenia, Barbados to New Zealand, suggests schools add a "Friendship Bench" to their garden to help students find friendly ways of resolving conflict. Students are encouraged to leave their resentments outside of the garden and discuss their concerns on the bench. Some schools are adapting the idea for indoor winter use, with quiet games, soft furniture, music and lighting, even student-made afghans and quilts. Morton-Marr says it can be helpful to give bullies the responsibility of garden design, creation, maintenance and promotion. Indoor plants could be used in the garden and moved to the outdoor garden in the spring.

Many wildlife, environmental, horticultural and charity organizations offer assistance for school gardens, including those listed in this book's Resources section.

It is clear that bullying is a school problem. Schools are where the kids are, most of the time. Schools are where the bullies reign, most of the time. And schools are where the solution lies—it's the only feasible place. We can ask parents to improve their child-rearing techniques—monitor their kids better, discipline them more consistently— but that is not realistic. Not all parents are willing, or able, to make that effort. In fact, few of the parents whose kids are really causing trouble would be inclined to read this book. But schools can make a difference: children are their captive audience. What's necessary is the collective will and support to make that happen. Teachers today are under incredible stress: battered by politics, by bureaucracy, by children who are increasingly out of control. Asking them to go above and beyond the crowded curricula to solve a deep-seated problem like bullying is a little overwhelming and can't be done—not without an entirely new philosophy on the part of decision-makers and holders of the public and private purse-strings. The above suggestions offer a start. But don't expect dramatic results. Bullies have been ruling playgrounds forever and they won't give up their crowns overnight. But patience and commitment can shorten their reign of terror. And in the long run, given time to change schools' and society's deep-seated attitudes, we may one day bring peace to childhood.

7

The Bully in Society

Carole has a 16-year-old son who is a bully with a shaved head and a knife in his pocket. Almost every day she racks her brain trying to figure out what went wrong. However, it doesn't make sense, she says, to wonder "whatever happened to Johnny," minutely inspecting him and their family, without also looking at the thousands of other kids with knives. Not to shirk the blame or anything, but the world has changed.

Carole feels that in the "old days" kids used to know, whether through osmosis or heated dinnertime discussion, how dad and mom voted, whether they were pro-union or anti-whatever and why they believed what they did. Not any more, Carole says. Parents are too busy trying to make ends meet. Kids are swamped with messages from the media and their friends. She shakes her head. "Kids don't know what to believe in. They have nothing to tie into, no morals or values they can

> *agree or disagree with. They've got so much free-*
> *dom but they don't have the equipment to deal*
> *with that freedom responsibly."*

Bullies don't live in isolation. They live in an aggressive world, and to a certain extent they owe their identity to that world, a world of name-calling politicians, bullying rap stars, rude wrestling heroes and radio and talk-show hosts who get paid to embarass others verbally.

It's a macho world, rife with bullies. A world dominated by the media, materialism and the philosophy of winner-takes-all.

That's why it doesn't work for parents who try to isolate themselves in a fantasy land of gentle values. Parents may reassure themselves by saying, "Where I live, the other kids who my kids are allowed to play with, the way I look after my family—this will protect them from bullies." They're fooling themselves. All the enthusiasm and commitment in the world may be wasted effort if it is focused solely on the problem at hand and the underlying causes are not addressed.

The individual teacher or parent can't hope to make a dent in a local bullying problem without looking at the bigger picture, at the bully in society. If we want to wipe out pint-sized aggression, then we've got to curb grown-up aggression too.

OUR AGGRESSIVE WORLD

Changing attitudes is a difficult task, given that the bully's kick-butt mentality is as pervasive as it is. In fact that may be part of the problem: the manifestations of aggression are so prevalent that we've become hopeless and apathetic. Everywhere young, developing minds turn they see self-centered adults striving for success, power-hungry, competing to get ahead. They see respectable grownups who have merely replaced bullying with their fists with bullying with their money or their minds. They see their country's leaders name-calling and shooting insults under the guise of criticism. They see the competitive outlook continually reinforced, from the casual card game to the piano recital to the child's classroom. As Gore Vidal has said, "It is not enough to succeed. Others must fail." And their little minds absorb.

Because their sense of right and wrong is not yet fully developed, kids can't understand why society says it's okay to bomb a bunch of people in Serbia but it's not okay to kill one person in a grocery store. Why does one killer go to jail, the other gets a medal? How can we expect our kids not to be bullies when our leaders draw lines in the sand and dare others to cross, pointing out, over and over again, that might means right?

One-upmanship is woven through our culture. A baseball game can't end until there's a winner and a loser. It's a fact of life. Whether in school or in the work force, everyone bullies or is bullied in some way at some time or another.

It's also clear what side society is on. It is inherent in our culture to dislike victims. We love leaders, renegades and rebels. We love the credo "No guts, no glory." And it follows that if you have no guts, you have no status either. A person who isn't tough and strong is a complainer. A chicken. A wimp. As Max Jackson, school principal and teacher in the Peace Department at McMaster University puts it, "The world needs a macho-ectomy."

As a society, we tend to disbelieve victims or we blame their problems on them. A child is beaten up for his lunch money and complains to the teacher. The teacher may respond: "Stand up for yourself" or demand, "What were you doing over there in the big boys' section?" In other words, what did you do to provoke it? On an adult level, a rape victim must defend herself in the courtroom, explain why she wore that particularly provocative dress, why she went to that bar, slept with those men in her past. The victim must have done *something* to make him assault her.

Some believe materialism, carried to an extreme in North American culture in recent years, is a form of bullying too. A society that seeks immediate gratification—"I want it now and I'm going to go out and get it now"—sends another pro-bully message to its younger generations.

"We've taken the Me Generation to a different level without realizing the fallout," says one youth counsellor. Today's family is a collection of individuals, everyone with his or her own distinct roles, classes, clubs, team practices. Few activities are undertaken by the family as a unit any more. Because the influence not only of the family but of school, community and church has diminished, kids end up having to make their own rules with the help of only the media and friends.

THE BULLY IN THE MEDIA

Boris admits he started the whole thing by calling another child a name. His victim didn't back down. Boris stepped up his verbal attack. The name-calling escalated. In the playground the other students' radar sensors, tuned to excitement, sounded the warning. Like moths to a light,

they gathered around. Soon there was no way out
for either child. They were surrounded by a tight,
adrenalin-filled circle. The kids started pushing
the two boys towards each other, shouting "Fight,
fight." Of course, they did.

"Why did the kids do that?" Boris, a hulking boy
who is new to Canada, wonders later. Maybe it's
because they like to watch fights, he says. He has
discovered that in this country fighting is enter-
tainment, like the fights people watch on TV, only
a little more exciting because this time it's real.

Boris is absolutely right. Television is a huge part of children's lives today, and fighting is a huge part of television.

Through the media, children have a window on the
adult world and, for the most part, the image they get is
of a paranoid, retaliatory place where actual war looks
amazingly like a Nintendo game. Fantasy heroes are
tough guys. Watch them fall off cliffs! Shoot their guns!
Nab the druggies! Get it in instant replay and even slow
motion! There are programs filled with bad people and
bad things happening. Thanks to the media, children are
bombarded by bullies, day in, day out.

Try as they might, parents can't escape. Even a fun
little family outing to the fast-food joint is infected when
Junior must have those cute little Gungan toy creatures
from *Star Wars: The Phantom Menace*. While his body
consumes the french fries, his mind consumes a slick
marketing message for a laser gunfire-laced hit movie.

And so that safe little segment of life called childhood
is wiped out. Thanks to modern media—television,
movies, music, video games and the Internet—kids are
free to float in and out of adulthood, privy to all its dirty

secrets. Traumatized and desensitized, they end up viewing the world as a dangerous place where you can't count
on adults to protect you. You're on your own.

> *"I felt horrible, scared, nowhere to turn." One*
> *victim describes her days at the hands of a bully.*
> *"You keep taking it 'til you can't stand it any*
> *more. You try to be nice and avoid it, dodge it,*
> *whatever it takes. But being bullied has taught me*
> *that it's time to teach children, from an early age,*
> *individual self-respect and kindness to others,*
> *common decency and human dignity. An image of*
> *rough and tough boys and demure girls doesn't do*
> *anyone any good. Our cartoons, commercials and*
> *videos don't help much. It's a circular argument:*
> *where do you begin, the home or the media?"*

Ideally, you fight the bully war on both fronts. And the
first battle can take place on the family-room sofa, in front
of the TV, where you'll find a good many young people
today because they're bored, because their parents are
busy, or simply because. In our increasingly obese and
indulgent society, it's the easiest way to kill some time.
In fact one study found most 4 to 6-year-olds surveyed
would rather watch TV than spend time with their dads.[1]
Statistics reveal that kids spend more time watching television than in any other waking activity; by the time
they're 15, they'll have spent more hours in front of the
tube than in school.

During that time they will have witnessed about 8,000
murders and 100,000 other acts of violence. Many will
have watched the play-by-play news of mass murders,
Pulp Fiction and *Natural Born Killers* on the VCR, music

videos with violent themes. And many will have spent a good part of their childhood waging a silent war with the video-game machine, an addictive pastime that packs a powerful punch. Young players assume the role of a hero who overcomes obstacles; the more spontaneous and aggressive the encounter, the better the youth feels when he succeeds. It's not a big leap to practice those lessons in the school yard.

VIDEO GAMES THAT KILL FOR FUN

Remember Pong, the first video game that shook the world in the 1970s? It took hours to hook up to the TV, but when dad finally figured out where all the plugs went, boy was it worth it! To see that little white ball bounce off the sides of the TV-screen—talk about excitement!

We've come a long way. Twenty-six years later, games are intricate and intense. They open worlds and work the brain. They are also, unfortunately, often violent and frighteningly similar to those used by the military to train soldiers to kill. The bigger the body count, the better the buzz.

And few families escape this pervasive new form of entertainment. Surveys from the National Institute on Media and the Family show video and computer games are among children's most asked for gifts during the Christmas holidays. Sixty-nine per cent of parents report their children own or rent games, mostly between the ages of eight and 12. Kids who play the games do so an average of seven hours per week. A 1998 study found that almost 80 per cent of games preferred by kids had violence or aggression as part of the play—much of it directed toward the other characters.[2]

The institute believes most games on the market are fine for kids and, in fact, seem to be getting better. There is concern, however, about the "ultra-violent" games. In fact, "games" is a bit of a misnomer. "Kill-for-fun murder simulations," Dr. David Walsh, the institute's president, calls them. These products are gory and lurid and require the use of increasingly intense violence to move through various levels of "play," severing limbs and spurting blood in the process. Unfortunately this group of games is very popular with kids and is marketed directly at them, with such inspiring slogans as "More fun than shooting your neighbor's cat" and "as easy as killing babies with axes." In its surveys, the institute found that most parents do not know the content of their children's games, nor do they consult the ratings in deciding whether to allow their kids to rent or buy them. As well, many children are sampling ultra-violent games off the Web, unhampered by rating systems which are, for the most part, ignored.

What this all means is still unclear. Because violent video games are relatively new, the research is still sparse. So far, though, researchers have uncovered some disturbing trends:

- Five-to-seven-year-olds imitated during free play what they had just been exposed to on video games, with the children who played the violent games showing more aggression.[3]
- In three different studies (four-to-six-year-olds, seven-to-eight-year-old boys and Grade 5 girls), aggressive behavior increased after they played or watched someone else play a violent video game.[4]
- After playing a very violent video game, children ascribed more hostile motives to others than did children who had just played a non-violent video game.[5]

It's true that some good does come from the media. One study found that TV may be an important source of learning for high-IQ children. Gifted kids like learning in an unstructured, flexible way and quality TV programs fit the bill.[6] There are also indications that children become more kind and considerate when they watch programs that demonstrate kindness and consideration for others.

Still, the evidence is piling up against television. An increasing number of social scientists and children's health professionals, including the American Academy of Pediatrics, the American Psychological Association, two U.S. Surgeon-General reports and the Ontario Medical Association's Committee on Child Welfare, warn that TV can be bad. Hundreds of studies and reviews support the idea that exposure to TV violence increases the likelihood of aggressive or antisocial behavior, particularly in males.

With that in mind, it might be best to err on the side of caution, to assume that all this videogazing has to have at least some negative effects and likely contributes in some degree to schoolyard bullying.

HOW TELEVISION AND MOVIE VIOLENCE IS DIFFERENT TODAY

An 11-year-old boy brags about seeing Nightmare on Elm Street *alone when he was five years old. He wasn't even afraid, he boasts. What was his secret? "It was easy. I pretended I was Freddy Kruger. Then I wasn't scared. Now that's what I always do and I'm never scared."*

Freddy Kruger is the villain of *Nightmare on Elm Street*, a monster who destroys his victims in an incredibly gory way. This is not the Road Runner and Coyote. There's blood and flesh and dead bodies everywhere. It's a new breed of media violence that leaves little to the imagination and little escape for impressionable minds.

In movies of the past, acts of aggression used to be performed by the bad guy and the bad guy never got away, at least not without being penalized. True, the old cowboy and Indian movies were pretty violent, but it was a sanitized and remote violence; viewers would hear a gun and watch someone fall off his horse, but the victim would be several hundred feet away from the camera.

Now, violence caters to the darker side of human nature: it is more frequent, performed by the hero just as often as the villain and the brutality is often free of consequence. It is sanitized and glamorized, unpunished and unjustified. It's often not only gratuitous to the plot but is also seen in close up, realistically accurate in every detail. Thanks to today's technology, you can be there.

And even the youngest of the young can be there. With the widespread domestic use of VCRs, satellite dishes and cable, children have unprecedented access to material intended for adults. Experts say 73 to 89 per cent of programs watched by Canadian children contain aggressive behavior. Kids as young as Grades 4 and 5 report having seen the gruesome *Silence of the Lambs* and surveys have revealed that kindergarten-aged children are big fans of the *Terminator* movies, bang-up affairs riddled with shootings, killing sprees and state-of-the art weaponry. The latest high-tech weaponry craze has been for the *Star Wars* sequel, a virtually plot-free, dialogue-free celebration of enemy elimination that is propelled by an aggressive, expensive marketing machine targeting North American children.

The record-breaking movie *Jurassic Park* left many adults cringing, but children seem proudly immune. They're often proud of the fact that they weren't scared by the blood and guts, that they didn't look away from the screen once (while mom covered her eyes and dad held his stomach). What does this say about the media's effects on our children?

Researchers Sandra Campbell and Jo-Anne Corbeil

spent 18 months interviewing 75 children ages eight to 14 to find out how electronic entertainment has affected them. They were chilled by the results. The researchers found most children watched as much as four hours per day of television and videos made for adults, and what they were watching was extremely violent, from fictional dramas to *America's Most Wanted* and *Rescue 911*.

These children were fearful a lot of the time but they were isolated in their fear, anxious to avoid being perceived as sissies or being ridiculed by their peers. At the same time, they were struggling with a "huge baggage load of gruesome images in their heads," Campbell says.[7]

Their heroes were most often Arnold Schwarzeneggar and Jean-Claude Van Damme, males in a male world who earn their status through brute force. These guys have zero interpersonal skills. Faced with conflict, they simply blow the enemy away. They are role models whose violent behavior is presented as glamorous and without consequence.

THE MEDIA'S EFFECTS ON BEHAVIOR

Dawn remembers coming home to find her ten-year-old son Jeff and his friends watching The Texas Chainsaw Massacre *on the VCR. Jeff was white as a sheet and suffered nightmares for weeks after. But he never let anyone know that the violence bothered him; the peer pressure to act tough was too strong. So he kept on watching brutal movies and kept his mouth shut.*

Fast forward five years: Jeff's grandma, who thinks the sun sets on her precious grandson, buys him a Chicago Bulls jacket, although Jeff's

*mother warns her against it. Jeff arrives home
from school, his nose broken, his face smashed
up. "Look, ma. Look at me," he smiles through the
blood. "And I still got it!" waving the jacket he
had managed to hang on to. His mother doesn't
directly blame the* Massacre-*like movies for the
violence in her son's life today, but nonetheless
she thinks there might be a link.*

Experts say there is. Studies indicate that media violence
is a problem, not so much because young people imitate
it but for more subtle reasons. They say the constant,
brutal bombardment of aggression has several effects.

- It wears down a child's resistance to violence.
- It subverts his values.
- It dulls his sensitivity to victim suffering.

Extensive TV viewing at an early age is associated with
less self-control and more aggressive behavior at later
ages. Several studies saw children who, after watching a
violent show, were slower to intervene or call for help
when they saw younger children fighting or being
destructive. Another study found that at age 30, the
person who watched a lot of TV violence when they
were eight will have more convictions for violence, more
arrests for drunken driving, be more aggressive under the
influence of alcohol and be more abusive toward their
spouse. They'll also have more aggressive children.[8]

According to Leonard Eron, professor of psychology
and research scientist at the Institute for Social Research
in Michigan, television spreads its violence indiscrimi-
nately—boys and girls of all ages, socio-economic levels

and intelligence are affected. Kids get stuck in a vicious cycle, he says. The violence they watch makes them more aggressive and then to justify their aggressive behaviour, they turn to watching more violence.[9]

Other studies have linked TV habits with school performance: families that have the TV on during meals or even when no one is watching, whose kids frequently watch TV before bed or copy characters they have seen on TV, are more likely to report poor school performance. [10]

There are many parents who believe their children won't be affected because the violence they watch is supposedly clean. There's no blood or gore in Pokemon or the World Wrestling Federation, for example. What could be wrong with it? Plenty. When violence isn't messy, kids get the message that violence is a great pain-free way to solve conflict. It simply shows kids that violence has no consequence except eliminating your enemy and the lesson is swiftly transferred to the playground at recess.

The other big problem with shows like *Batman* and *Beast Wars* is that the bad guys never really go away. They keep coming back for more. The good guy doesn't win; he gets a temporary reprieve until the next episode. Videogames are disturbing for the same reason.

Particularly disturbing to child development experts are the shows that depict a victim who finally snaps, like Leonardo DiCaprio's character in the 1995 movie *The Basketball Diaries* who guns down his classmates in revenge, or Michael Douglas's 1993 movie *Falling Down*, in which the audience has some sympathy for the hero's violent behavior. Since Douglas's and DiCaprio's characters had a hard time of it, it's all right if they're a bit brutal. This kind of attitude adds fuel to the fire of the high-school vigilantes who seek revenge on bullies.

MEDIA VIOLENCE: NOVOCAINE FOR THE MIND

"My ten-year-old watches violent movies all the time and it doesn't bother him," one mother says with pride. She wonders if that means her son is exceptionally mature, that he can deal with disturbing movies and not be upset. Just the contrary, psychologists say. Violence *should* bother children. The fact that it doesn't means her son may have built up a hard, unhealthy veneer. This mom should worry.

Many experts believe that a couch-potato child may become a couch potato for life, numb to life's injustices, passive, paralyzed by paranoia, unable to take part in the world around him. Children who are insecure in other ways—overly aggressive or unable to form close bonds—may be most affected by the violence.

A child learns by playing, exploring and experimenting. By taking part in the world around him, the well-adjusted child learns that his behavior has consequences; he discovers that he can have an effect on his world. But when children watch TV, they are powerless. While they are passively sucking in the images on the screen for several hours a day, they are missing out on those healthy lessons. And when they are taking in violent fare, especially the Ninja Turtle kind where danger lurks behind every corner, limitless and invincible, experts say young minds begin to believe that the world is a dangerous place and they are powerless to defend themselves.

Children absorb a "mean world syndrome" which revolves around who gets away with what against whom. Alienated and suspicious, heavy viewers may go in one of two different directions: they may begin to show a high amount of anxiety and apprehension in their lives, fearing that this is a violent world and one you can't trust. Experts say they may start to identify themselves as victims because much of the violence in the media is shown from the victim's viewpoint. Or they can adopt the dog-eat-dog attitude of aggression, believing that the only way to survive in this world is to look out for Number One.

Some research shows that aggression on television can have the most damaging effect on troubled kids, children who have been neglected or abused early in life. These insecurely attached children feel isolated, lack trust and are unable to form healthy relationships.

And there is evidence that violence in the media has the most effect on kids who have a predisposition to violence. For this reason, it is important to teach children social skills early, as a kind of protective armor, so that they are not as vulnerable to imitating the behavior they see on violent shows.

But even though parents may tell children that what they are watching is not real, the message doesn't register with young children. Until the age of 7 or 8, research shows, children are concrete thinkers, which makes it very difficult for them to distinguish between fantasy and reality. When they are told that what they're seeing on TV is "just pretend," they may nod in agreement with the words. Unfortunately, what is in front of them on the screen is much more impressive than mere words and that's what they believe. They are unable to rationalize away what they see. Because they are concrete thinkers, what they see is taken literally, especially with today's special effects. This leaves them exceptionally vulnerable to the effects of TV violence.

A child's world is a world of fantasy and imagination.

Children become so caught up in their fantasies that the line between television and reality is easily blurred and the antisocial TV models that they watch every day are incorporated into their imaginative play.

THE BULLY IN NON-VIOLENT TV

It's not only the violent schlock that worries child psychologists. Situation comedies, dramas and cartoons can have negative effects too.

A lot of a child's TV watching is done in the evenings, when mom and dad are exhausted and trying to recover from their busy day. Prime-time for children, between 4:00 p.m. and 9:00 p.m., is when much of the mind garbage is aired: the old made-for-TV cop-chasing re-runs, the eyewitness tabloid shows with live or life-like violence, the confrontational talk shows and the dramas that feature tense, unhappy characters and ominous, anxiety-producing soundtracks.

Even ostensibly non-violent shows often demonstrate a mean streak, a peculiar sort of psychological violence. Talk shows are the modern equivalent of the carnival freak show, where everyone gets to gang up on some poor lost soul who has, for some unfathomable reason, agreed to be humiliated in public. The show's guest—usually a misfit who has done something weird or different or not very nice—is cornered on stage while the host and the audience bully him in front of the world. Great sport.

The same "all-in-good-fun" defense is thrown about by obnoxious radio announcers like Howard Stern. Stern, North America's bully of the airwaves, is hugely popular with young people who revel in his blatantly abusive behavior of minority groups. When Stern trivializes others' pain, as he has with groups like the Kosova refugees and victims of the Littleton school shootings, he models really rotten behavior in the guise of harmless fun.

And situation comedies are often far from gentle. The more popular sit-coms feature a machine-gun barrage of barbs and put-downs. Children watch family members ridicule each other in *Married With Children*, they witness Roseanne Barr's rough and gruff parenting, they cheer along with the ill-mannered rebellious Bart Simpson, and learn that silicone breast implants guarantee popularity in *Student Body*. In show after show they watch obnoxious or precocious kids verbally sniping at each other, hurling one-liners and smart-alecky, sarcastic insults to a background of canned laughter that emphasizes jokes made at the expense of someone else.

In recent years in North America, public pressure has succeeded in setting new laws that encourage more educational children's television and discourage gratuitous violence. Much of what is aimed at children today has been cleaned up somewhat; even that old meanie *Power Rangers* runs "feel-good" trailers at the end of each show. But what is of growing concern to many experts is the huge proliferation of channels, the penetration of cable in the U.S., and increased choice available to children. Kids no longer watch just the kid stuff. They are tuning into "adult animated" shows like *South Park* which offer inappropriate language and activity, adult-oriented shows like *Jerry Springer*, and the local news all of which present a distorted, mean and violent view of the world. They hear about people they trusted, priests and school principals, facing sex assault charges. They watch their leaders bomb Eastern Europe and learn that it's okay to kill certain people—as long as they are the bad guys. And everywhere they are doused with in-your-face culture, from *Beavis and Butt-head* to Just-Do-It/Bite-Me attitude advertisements.

"There have always been and there always will be kids drawn to extreme behavior," explains David Walsh, president of the National Institute on Media and the Family. "But what qualifies as extreme is related to the definition of normal. If normal behavior is kids treating each other with some respect, then the extreme might be a verbal outburst, a kick or a punch. But if put-downs and 'in your face' behavior is already the norm...threat and intimidation...then the extreme behavior is going to go farther over the edge."

> *Mom rushes into the family room to switch off the TV. Her children are watching their favorite cartoon characters shoot each other with the latest cartoon-tech weaponry. Such violent fare is a no-no in this household. "No, wait, Mom," the eldest child yelps. "You'll like this—the reason they're killing them is for peace."*

It would be funny if it weren't so serious. But many of today's cartoons aren't funny at all. If they weren't sugar-coated in animation, their violent content would probably floor even the most hardened TV watcher and send any parent scurrying to the "off" button.

> *Saturday morning and you're sleeping in. How nice that Katie and Mark have figured out how to turn the TV on themselves. How nice that there are cartoons and appropriate programs for them in the morning. Roll over and go back to sleep,*

*blessing the box that babysits on sleepy mornings
like this.*

Don't sleep too soundly. You may be surprised to learn that
Saturday morning children's TV is a grotesque ghetto of
aggression. Granted, there are some good programs, like
Barney and Friends and the venerable *Sesame Street.* But if
you can make yourself sit through one Saturday morning's
fare, you'll discover that a lot of of theoretically harmless
cartoons are anything but. Besides sex-role stereotyping,
there's a plethora of mind-numbing, violent escapades. The
old Roadrunner was nothing compared to some of these
malicious monsters, mutants and heroes. You may think
your children are safe watching peaceful shows, but that's
not necessarily so: during commercial breaks they may be
bombarded with loud teeth-gnashing ads for action toys
and promos for upcoming violent programs.

Switch the TV off and kids pick up their action toys,
bashing them, zapping them, using force and aggression
according to a script they've learned on the tube. Their
play has become narrowly defined according to the
cartoon- and toy-makers—often one and the same. True,
kids have always had cowboys and Indians and GI Joes,
but not to this degree, not with the kind of advertising
pressure and intensification that we have today. At a very
young age our children are learning to be consumers,
learning that they must have the latest Pokemon figure,
the tear-away or cargo pants, the best-marketed running
shoe, the latest Guess/Gap/Hilfiger/Club Monaco fad.
Little girls wobble around on Spice-Girl-high platform
runners—eight-year-old fashion snobs. Experts worry
that this becomes an acquisitiveness that verges on bullying—the person who has the most stuff has the most

power—and that has the strongest effect on those with weakest self-esteem.

When we let the advertisers and cartoon creators baby-sit our children, we let them teach our children too. And quite often what they're learning builds up the ominous, omnipotent bully in society. One way to fight back may be to take control of the remote control and a stronger interest in your child's media consumption.

TIPS FOR PARENTS: HOW TO BATTLE THE TV BULLY

One-and-a-half-year-old Jake and his three-year-old brother Jordie are motionless on the family-room couch, their eyes fixed on the television screen. The Joker is racing around Gotham City, doing his best to blow Batman away. Dad sees nothing wrong with what his preschoolers are watching. All kids are into Batman and Pokemon, he says. Jake and Jordie would be seen as oddballs if they weren't into them too.

A well-educated man, this father concedes there may be some truth to the theory that aggressive movies beget aggressive kids. But he says he's not going to try a social experiment on his children by forbidding them to watch. If he did, he worries his children would be less aggressive than their peers, little wimps wide open to bullying. It's his way of protecting them, he explains, against an aggressive world.

It's tough to step away from the crowd. Especially when you're only three-foot-two. That's why mom and dad need to be the strong ones, the ones who take a stand.

Smart TV viewing needn't make your child a wimp. But it may keep him from being a bully.

The earlier you start fostering good habits, the easier it will be. In fact, parents would be wise to start monitoring and rationing TV at the preschool age, because once children enter school there is incredible peer pressure to watch what's popular. Here are some suggestions to help battle the boob-tube bully.

- If used properly, TV can be a powerful and positive learning tool. That is, when parent and child watch together, after chores and homework are done, after a calm negotiation has taken place to determine what can be watched and when.
- Handing your child the remote control can amount to handing your child a loaded gun, experts say. Rather than allowing him to channel-hop wherever he likes, help him create his own personal TV guide. Every Saturday, plan the week's viewing. Delve through the TV listings, deciding together what is okay to watch, then copy the choices onto a separate sheet of paper labelled "My Personal TV Guide." Or have each family member circle their choice on the listings with different-colored pens. You can leave this guide with babysitters when you go out, so they can clearly see what shows you consider appropriate.
- Don't let your under-eight child watch TV news—it's often gruesome, explicit, and leaves them feeling angry, depressed and scared. Network news coverage of homicides in the United States leaped by 336 per cent between 1990 and 1995, even though the homicide rate dropped by 13 per cent.[11] If your older child

watches the news, watch it with him and switch it off if it's disturbing.

- Limit TV to one or two hours (or less) a day. Or limit it to the weekend, taping shows during the week that you want to watch on Saturday or Sunday.
- You may want to allow "bonus" shows, educational programs on public broadcasting stations that children can watch over and above their allotted TV-watching time
- Point out how quickly tough issues get settled on TV and ask your children if they think that in real life these problems would be solved in 30 minutes, minus commercial time.
- Point out how the laugh track or the music or the editing is used to manipulate emotions.
- Talk to them about special effects and trick photography. By the age of eight or nine, kids should be able to tell what is real and what isn't and begin to develop a healthy skepticism about what they're watching.
- Because violence is such an entrenched part of our society, you may want to watch the occasional violent program with your kids and talk about it, rather than ban aggressive shows altogether. Ask them how many acts of violence they're witnessing. Get them to tell you what's real and what's not. Ask them if there are other, gentler ways of resolving difficulties. Have they thought about what would happen if a TV program eliminated all the violence?
- Use a violent program as an opportunity to discuss issues it may raise, such as human rights, values, right and wrong, and might means right.
- Give your children regular, caring, adult guidance to

help them learn the real-life negative consequences of the bullying behavior they see their heroes enacting. Serve as a role model, demonstrating the full range of human feelings and healthy actions to counteract the negative stuff they may take in through the media.

- Kids can have fun learning how actors simulate violence and create special effects. You can create your own family-room theater with your children, acting out different methods of solving the same problem in the TV world and the real world.

- When violence occurs on television, don't sneer, "That's junk." This will only create a gap between you and your child. Instead, let him know that kind of aggressive behavior makes you uncomfortable.

- Switch a show off if it is particularly violent or offends you, and let advertisers know you've switched it off. Studios and networks may change their tune when consumers make advertisers concerned about shows that glamorize violence.

- If you turn off the television, don't then make the children do chores. Any TV show can't help but look attractive compared to cleaning out the garage. Give your child a more appealing alternative, something they can do with you such as reading a book, baking cookies or going shopping.

- Don't let your children have a television in their bedroom—it makes it too difficult to monitor what, and how often, they are watching. One study found 39 per cent of eight-to-12-year-olds and 56 per cent of 13-to-17-year-olds have televisions in their bedrooms, despite the fact that bedroom sets are linked to more TV-watching and more negative effects on behavior.[12]

- Ask your child if she likes the show she is watching

and how it makes her feel. Listen, respectfully, to her
answer, then offer your opinion.

BOOST YOUR INTERNET INTELLIGENCE

We warn our children to stay away from dangerous people
and situations, and yet many of us allow our kids to hole themselves up in a room for hours while they delve into the Internet.
There's no point in restricting a child's TV watching, then giving
him unrestricted access to the Web—it can be just as dangerous, maybe more so. For a vulnerable, shy or hurting child, the
Internet can be a suicidal sinkhole. Keep the computer in a well-
traveled room in the house, and poke your head in the door
frequently. Learn how to access the History file to discover what
they've been doing, and make use of systems that enable you
to monitor and restrict their Website wandering.

BULLIES AND THE SPORTING LIFE

*The TV announcer raises his voice in excitement
as the basketball players forget the ball and turn
on each other. "They're going at it; it's a brawl!"
He oozes enthusiasm. This, of course, is what
everyone loves to see. Nothing like raw emotion
and a few good pileups to get the audience going.*

The sports world can be another big source of aggression
for today's youth. The increasing violence in games like
hockey blurs the lines between bullying and sports. Little
ones raised to tackle and bodycheck their opponents can
assume bullying is fair play. As far as the child is
concerned, the playground bully is just participating in
another contact sport.

The problem is that, when children are encouraged to
use violent behavior in sports, it's difficult for them to

turn off that behavior when they leave the field or rink. They can no longer tell what's appropriate and what's not. Their sports are violent, so violence becomes sport.

The biggest roar at a hockey game occurs when a fight breaks out on the ice. It seems this is what the spectators want. But when children see adults doing it on TV, studies show, it legitimizes violence for them. They learn how to play the game violently by watching their heroes and then practicing it themselves.

> *The scene: another basketball game. One of the players throws an intimidating, adrenaline-laden stare at one of the opposing players. The spectators hold their breath; they know this is going to lead to something exciting, and of course it does. The coach excuses the melee later with a shrug: "If the guy has any get up and go, that's gotta upset him."*

The influence of sports on everyday life is even stronger today because sports figures are heroes and celebrities. Because they are so high-profile, the media focuses on their fights as never before. And with the sky-high salaries and major media events, there is more money involved in sports. That leads to more competition, more antagonism, more aggression. When sports stars can be bullies, popular and rich all at once, what's to stop our kids from thinking they can try it too?

After the Colorado tragedy (where jocks were blamed for bullying and targeted by the bullied gunmen), criticism turned to the athlete-is-king attitude that festers in many schools. But even before the tragedy, concern was growing over the link between sports and violence. By 1995, high school basketball games in the Toronto area had reached a low point: coaches had been stabbed, bottles were thrown in stands and fistfights were breaking out at the drop of a baseball cap. There were calls for coaches to put more emphasis on sportsmanship and less on winning games. A whole host of initiatives followed to try to change attitudes and put fun back into school sports. One area, for example, held a frisbee competition in which kids made the rules and the winning team presented roses to all the female participants.

Leagues developed codes of behavior aimed at athletes, coaches and spectators. At many schools, the MVP award was replaced with an award for the player who shows the best fair play and sportsmanship. In some areas, a team sportsmanship award is being presented at a special school assembly several days after the competition, so that the significance is not lost in the excitement over the tournament's high score winner.

The sports world continues to battle the Dennis Rodman-ish attitude where winning is everything and nice guys finish last. But slowly the gap is growing between the money-focused world of the professionals and the more fun-loving, less elite world of amateur sports.

BOYS WILL BE BOYS

It's a beautiful, early spring day at the neighborhood park. Moms and tots have shucked their coats and flocked to the playground. In the sand pile, a group of girls is playing make-believe, quietly acting out elaborate scenes: house and hair-dos and holding hands. But all around this quiet little theater, hell is breaking loose. Two boys are racing around, shouting insults and shooting at each other with sticks. And over by the swings a couple of older boys are taunting a smaller one, making fun of him because he's afraid to jump from the highest bar.

The old snails-and-puppy-dog-tails rhyme may be politically incorrect, but not altogether wrong. As any boy's parent will attest, behind that cherubic mud-streaked face there's often an aggressive little ruffian clambering to get out—a macho, macho man.

It's a well-known fact that males are behind much of the crime carried out in this world. According to Statistics Canada, of the 18,800 charges laid against youths aged 12 to 17 in 1991 in Canada, 82 per cent were laid against boys. Studies show that boys demand more violent entertainment. And boys bully more.

Is it all testosterone or is there something else behind the trouble? It's possible there are other factors at work. Male adolescents lag behind females in their development and that can present problems for some boys. During this awkward time, they may be fearful of and confused by strong new emotions and find it tough to support the old macho myths. This affects their self-esteem and they go for intense peer bonding to get it back again. Searching for a role model, they find it in the violent heroes and the macho mythology presented by movies and TV and sports stars.

Another theory is that, because males don't have a lot of permission or encouragement in our society to talk about and acknowledge their feelings, they have a smaller repertoire of words and are more likely to act out their emotions. If a boy cries, he is told not to be a baby or a sissy. He is taught to define his maleness by being the opposite of female. Parents may love Mr. Rogers, the gentle host of the children's TV show, but would they want their boys to grow up like him? Few fathers would. There's something a little weird and intimidating about a guy who is so, well, *soft*.

Boys are raised to suppress their emotions and feelings of pain. This may leave them out of touch with their own feelings and unable to recognize their victim's pain. The victim's protests and suffering may simply not make any *sense* to them. As well, our society doesn't allow boys to be victims. It's a sissy thing; it calls into question their basic identity as a male human being. As a result, male victimization is much more under-reported than female victimization.

All this has a direct effect on bullying. If a boy is a victim, it is especially difficult because he feels he must keep his sense of inadequacy bottled up inside. It isn't manly to be victimized and if his dad ever found out, he'd be mortified. One boy, bullied in private school because he had skipped a grade and was younger, smaller, quieter and new to the school, says he tried to "take it like a man." He never told the authorities or his parents. After all, he was lucky enough to be attending this private school; admitting the problem would be admitting he'd failed and let his father down.

And if the boy is a bully, he may be following the lead of his heroes, believing he is doing what the world wants, acting like a macho man.

Parents, and society in general, can help boys cope with the macho myth.

- In their early years boys need to learn how to listen to their own feelings and express them verbally. It helps to have a male who can model healthy emotions for them. And it can help to ask them periodically, "How do you feel about that?" If the boy is acting in a macho way, with lots of bravado, ask him, "Are you feeling afraid? Why are you acting like that?" Boys need a guiding hand to help them interpret and question the messages the world is sending them.

- Children, boys especially, should be taught through role-modelling that just because they might be considered the dominant sex, the dominant culture or the dominant kid in the class doesn't mean they can use their power to bring others into line.

- Some rough-housing and rough and tumble are normal, especially among boys. But if, as an adult, you feel uncomfortable watching what's going on, stop it.

- Boys may benefit by having more male teachers, especially at the elementary-school level, to provide better role models. The primary influences on kids today are parents, school, TV and friends. If a boy is in a single-mother family or a family in which dad is busy working and all his teachers are women, then his role model will probably be someone like Bart Simpson or Bruce Lee or the tough guy who rules the playground. A kind, caring, successful male teacher can guide him down a better path.

A REASON TO HOPE

There is a bright light on the horizon.

The decade between 1975 and 1985 was "long and depressing" for Jim Deacove. He and his wife Ruth labored away in their old barn, designing and building cooperative games for an uninterested public. They felt they were alone in the wilderness. It seemed everyone was intent on beating everyone else; competition and aggression ruled.

But the Deacoves' work has finally found a market. Their cooperative games can be found on many store shelves and business is booming. Today's parents seem to be a little more sensitive, Jim Deacove explains. They are starting to realize that society needs to teach children better lessons. It's heartwarming and reassuring, he says, to discover this new collective psychological break-through, this societal insight that we can live together differently.

The growing popularity of cooperation-based games is a good sign that our aggressive world may be willing to be tamed. There are other good signs. A Gallup survey conducted in 1993 discovered that most Canadians are concerned about an increase in violence on TV. The poll found 72 per cent want to see limits on the amount of violence shown. More women than men (79 per cent versus 63 per cent) favored limits and most respondents said they believed television violence has increased over the past five years.

Also encouraging: there are new attempts to put a lid on TV violence that is graphic, glamorous or gratuitous. The V-chip, a device built into televisions to block unwanted programs, is finally on its way. In 1996 the telecommuni-cations act in the United States required new TVs to include the V-chip. Critics warn that V-chip is just a tech-nological Band-Aid, that it doesn't block news, sports and documentaries and that it will be used primarily by those who already monitor their kids' viewing.

But there are other efforts, from legislation to lawsuits,

that promise a major clean-up may be on the way.

Movie-makers say there has been a huge shift in attitude since the Colorado high school massacre. *The Basketball Diaries* and *Heathers*, movies that feature outcasts seeking revenge on their school, were both pulled from video store shelves across North America shortly after the shootings. Several high-profile TV series were scaled back or canceled. In June, several prominent Toronto casting directors refused to work on a teenage werewolf movie, saying they were revolted by the violence in the script. The massacre also prompted the U.S. government to set up a youth violence task force and studies into the marketing of violence to children with more than $1 billion directed into making youth safer. More than 50 prominent Americans have joined in an appeal to the entertainment industry to reduce violence, stop marketing violence to children, and establish minimum standards. Two influential United States senators have also introduced legislation that would require movie studios, record producers and video game makers to adopt a uniform rating system to label violent content, and establish fines as high as $10,000 a day for those who sell violent products to children. In addition, teens will have to produce photo identification cards to see R-rated movies at most U.S. theaters. In Canada, where movie classifications are under provincial jurisdiction, there have been calls for new classification codes.

Others hope to affect producers of media violence by hitting them in the pocketbook. In Louisiana, producer/director Oliver Stone, Time-Warner Entertainment and the distributors of Stone's 1994 movie, *Natural Born Killers*, are being sued by the estate of Patsy Ann Byers, who was shot by two youths allegedly re-enacting parts of the movie. Also worth watching are federal proceedings in Kentucky against Internet pornography providers, computer game manufacturers and the producers of the 1995 film *The Basketball Diaries*. This comes after a teenager allegedly acted out a classroom shooting scene.

Also, some of the biggest names on the Internet have joined with public interest groups to produce a Web site (www.getnetwise.com) that offers tips for safe surfing, sample contracts for children's Internet use, and information on filtering tools and on-line risks. U.S. gun producers have backed some of President Bill Clinton's key gun control proposals, including raising the gun ownership age from 18 to 21.

Across North America, political will to protect our kids is growing. Societal pressure is a powerful thing. It has already been proven that power can be marshalled and directed for the common good. Society is beginning to look down on smoking, drunk driving and sexism. There is hope that with a concerted effort, societal pressure can be harnessed once again to change attitudes, to turn against aggression, to remove the stigma on tattling and to take the bully off his pedestal.

While you're waiting for social attitudes to change, you can make changes in your own home by building your child's self-esteem. You can raise a non-victim by teaching him how to be assertive in this aggressive world.

WHAT SOCIETY CAN DO

Ironically, the U.S. doesn't seem to be as worried about bullying as other countries are, despite its high crime rate. The major thrust of research has come from Scandinavia, Europe and Japan, where aggression is relatively infrequent. There is speculation that bullying is regarded as worse in countries where it is not as entrenched. "We've become so desensitized to it here that it doesn't horrify us," says Dr. David G. Perry, professor of psychology at Florida Atlantic University.

The idea of changing our attitudes that are so deeply entrenched can seem a little overwhelming. It will take some time, but there are steps that society can take to dethrone the bully.

- Sports institutions can go after instigators of violence instantly, the minute it breaks out. Referees can step in sooner, with more penalties that send the clear message: violence will not be tolerated.
- Local parks and recreation departments could set up low-cost or free programs targeting high-risk youth, providing teens with a safe place to hang out.
- Federal governments can take the initiative by being the clearing house and funder of violence prevention programs to rectify the current piece-meal approach.
- Communities can set up weekly victim-support groups or a bullying hotline to give children anonymous access to adult counsellors.
- All adults, in every segment of society, should accept bullying as a community problem, give children constant feedback about their behavior and question violence on a small or large scale, whenever it occurs.
- An organized, cooperative, national plan of attack, which can deal with everything from keeping families together to fighting the abuse of power, may be what's necessary. A network of parents, media, educators and policy-makers could be organized to brainstorm ideas and solutions, treating aggression and violence as a community health issue and determining what families need to raise physically and emotionally healthy children.

8

Raising an Assertive— Not Aggressive—Child

Heather remembers when the aggressive boy next door started chasing her son around the yard. Before she knew it, the bully had her child pinned to the ground in a wrestling hold that his dad had taught him because, he said, "You need to know how to fight for yourself in this world." It hurt Heather incredibly to see the stunned helplessness on her son's face, to see the look in the eyes of her gently raised little boy as he reached up to her. It was an expression that said, "Why didn't you tell me about this? What am I supposed to do now?"

If you are like most parents, you are willing to do anything in your power to keep your children from feeling such pain. Is there something you can do? Is there some way to warn your child that it's not a bubble-gum world out there? And how do you tell him or her without bursting that protective little bubble that surrounds childhood and makes it so special?

AGGRESSIVENESS VERSUS ASSERTIVENESS

Many parents have tried to prepare their children, not always successfully.

One mother of a seven-year-old says, "My little boy knows that, when he does something to anyone else, he's going to get it twice as bad at home." (This child, incidentally, has been bullied by a schoolmate for the past two years.) Another parent has decided that he has the perfect approach for his son. He has instructed four-year-old Chris that if anyone should ever tease him or call him a name, he should just lay back and wallop him. That will make everyone know they'd better not mess with him.

Like many parents, this mother and father are grappling with that fine line between self-defence and bullying back, between assertiveness and aggressiveness. When *adults* find it hard to figure out the subtle difference between standing up for yourself and being a bully, just imagine how much muddier the picture looks to the enquiring minds of children.

It is especially difficult to prepare young boys. You can't help but worry: if you are too tough, will they be too rough? If you are too gentle, will they be wimps?

Some parents are reluctant to quell the aggressiveness in their children because they see it as healthy feistiness that will shield them from trouble. They like their kids to show a bit of spunk—even if they do lack respect, at least they've got spirit! One father confessed that he is teaching his children values that he doesn't believe in, fostering a tough, competitive outlook in them because he wants them to be able to cope in this dog-eat-dog world. The problem is, these parents may go a little light on the discipline. When a child is raised without firm limits, he will find it tough to live within limits as an adult. More importantly, he will never find the comfort in knowing that he is not on his own, that a more mature person who cares about his welfare is in control.

But it doesn't have to be that way. Self-esteem and assertiveness, built up gradually from babyhood on, are far more powerful, far better protectors. Instead of arming your child with machismo, you can arm him with a kind of brainy bravery, a calm, strong, intelligent demeanor that will keep him from being a bully or a victim and equip him with emotional immunity against the wayward blows of childhood.

One family, the Deacoves, took this philosophy to an extreme, sheltering their children from conflict and competition, giving them a uniquely pacifist upbringing and an entirely different view of the world. By the time these children discovered there were bullies out there, they had already built up armor to shield them from pain.

AN EXPERIMENT IN GENTLENESS

Jim and Ruth Deacove performed a kind of social experiment on their children, dropping out of the rat race and into their own rural utopia. They created a haven in a pastoral valley near the Quebec border, a commune where there was no competition, no sports, no TV and lots of talk.

By screening their two daughters from the negative noises bombarding the world outside their old farm-house, they hoped their children would grow up to be creative and non-aggressive, pacifists by nature yet strong enough to make it on their own.

Jim Deacove says they tried to treat their children

kindly at all times, willingly shared their possessions and gave them a firm foundation in caring for others and being secure in their own sense of self. "We believe our method taught them affection for themselves, helped them be secure about who they are, helped them find out what their interests and passions are. Then life takes care of them."

"We always had a say in how things went. We talked a lot, were treated as if we had opinions and what we said mattered," remembers one of the children, Tanya Deacove, now a trained art therapist. In fact, visiting other families in their homes was an eye opener, Tanya says. "I thought all families were like my family until I started making friends."

Until Grade 5, the two girls attended a private school set up on the commune. Between Grades 5 and 8 they were schooled at home by their parents. It wasn't until they attended public high school that they learned what the real world was like.

"Boy, I sure noticed things were different in the mainstream," Tanya recalls. "It was culture shock. I just watched. It was the intentional meanness, I think—the hypocrisy, how cruel everyone was, how competitive—that surprised me."

Tanya laughs remembering the way she handled bullies. "I think my pure innocence just blasted right through. I'd be in really scary situations but I didn't notice. I believed the best of people and gave them the opportunity to bring it out."

She and her sister Christa encountered a lot of teasing and bullying about being the crunchy granola alternatives from the valley. Tanya remembers the bus that took them to their high school in a nearby town. Like every school bus since school buses were invented, this one had a group of loud bullies lounging in the back, with the rest of the kids cowering as close to the driver as they could get.

"But I'd get on and say, 'Good morning, how are you?' to the bullies," Tanya recounts, "because that's the way I was raised—you send out good energy to people." She compares her behavior to a kitten who, not knowing any better, comes up and licks a big dog's nose. The bullies all shouted back at her that they were fine, making smart-aleck remarks that were supposed to sound tough and intimidating.

They didn't intimidate her, she says. "I saw bullies as really vulnerable people, as being scared. When you get really close to them, they run. They intrigued me."

Then one day Tanya got on the bus but wasn't feeling well, so she sat down quietly. The bullies missed her cheery hello. Out of the silence, one of the bullies' voices boomed forward, strangely rough and gentle at the same time. "Good morning, Tanya." She saw it as an offering of sorts, a kind of pat on the back to show that, beneath it all, they respected her for her quirky strength.

"That's a place I try to return to when I find myself getting afraid or being bullied," she says now. "I remind myself that I'm okay, that some other people just don't understand." She still struggles to find the assertiveness to stand up for herself, for the way she chooses to live. "It's hard not to be a doormat when you've been raised to be so gentle. I still wonder if I'm a weird alien. There's a real potential to get walked on.

"Sometimes I resent what my parents did. Because I never watched TV, I wasn't prepared for the aggressive-ness and competitiveness that is so much a part of our culture and society."

She remembers wanting to play competitive sports but her father wouldn't let her. This caused many arguments. "Geez, just wanting to play basketball made me feel as if I was contributing to a world war."

Yet she wants to instill those same values in her own children some day. Maybe she won't go to such an extreme. But she says being raised in a non-aggressive home gave her quiet strength. "I don't feel that I'm a wimp at all.... If you're really strong, you don't need to yell or scream at things, you can quietly persevere and speak out in a non-confrontational way."

Her new job, providing art therapy to abused kids, has shown her the starkly different world that some children face and has reinforced the lessons her parents taught her. "I see a lot of kids who've grown up in pretty abusive, violent families and they've got a lot of anger to let out. To me, that just reinforces how much we pass on to our children. When you hear about these kids beating other kids up at recess, you know they're just re-enacting scenarios they learned at home."

Using art therapy, Tanya allows children emotional expression that is both powerful and acceptable, helping them to direct their anger through art. It's part of her parents' legacy, Tanya says. "They've given me a seed of knowledge ... that you can live in a way that's better than the world is now. If you've had even a taste of what it can be like, then there's something in you that makes you want to keep going to make it a better place."

Jim Deacove admits it was a risky decision, especially when the girls got to high school and started to question their parents' approach. "We wondered, are they going to be too vulnerable? Are they going to be hurt?" They were fully aware they were performing a social experiment on their kids. "It takes a big leap of faith, no doubt about it. We worried that we were not equipping them to survive in the outside world. But we had a choice: do we give our children all the weaponry—intellectual and emotional—and add to the status quo, or do we make a commitment that we want to change society?

"After that, there was no choice.... We just couldn't add to the misery and pressure and so many things that contribute to mental-health problems in kids today."

For many parents, this approach may be a little too radical. But it holds lessons for us all. What the Deacoves managed to give their children was a strong self-image and a sense of self-worth. It can be the most effective shield against the bullies of this world.

While you can't bully-proof your child, you can, like the Deacoves, build up layer upon layer of self-confidence—layers of protective insulation—so that they feel safe, loved and competent, ready to take on the world without taking on the bully. If the developmental stages go well, then chances are that, when it becomes necessary, your child will be able to stand up for himself quietly and find ways to deal with bullying or to enlist the support he needs.

What's more, these strong emotional skills may help him to achieve success elsewhere in life. The ability to get along with people, empathize and make good personal decisions—what researchers call "emotional intelligence" (or EQ) may be more predictive of life success than the traditional IQ measurement. A high EQ has been linked with lower rates of delinquency, violence and drug use in children and more success later in life with their career, relationships and health.

HOW TO TOUGHEN UP YOUR CHILD

Sherry remembers being a shy, skinny little kid in Grade 4: "There was a girl in my class who was big and rough. One day she announced that she was going to take my new bike away. I told her she couldn't have it. This took place in front of everyone in the school yard. They all started chanting, 'Fight, fight, fight.'

"The girl grabbed my bike and demanded I give it to her. I said, 'No.' She said, 'Okay, we'll have to fight.' Nobody came to my defence. I put the bike down. I stared up at her and she down at me, for what seemed like forever. Suddenly she burst into tears and ran away.

"The crowd cheered and patted me on the back. I stood stunned and relieved. She never bothered me again. I learned a valuable lesson. Whether you are confronting bullies, ex-husbands or bank managers by yourself, quietly standing your ground is a strong offence. Much stronger than a weak defence."

Strength can take many forms. It takes strength not to run away crying; it takes strength not to flail back at the bully. It takes strength to do what Sherry did that day, to stand face-to-face with her fear. Bullies look for signs of weakness, be it whimpering, whining, crying or terrified flight from provocation. These are signs to the bully that her actions have had an effect, that she has demonstrated her power and dominance over another. Given such satisfaction, she'll try it again and again. Just as the bull charges a waving red flag, the bully charges a wavering self-image.

Not giving the bully what he wants takes great courage. Some parents erroneously believe that strength and courage come from being outwardly tough. Worried that their child is too soft and can't stand up to teasing, they run their own toughening-up campaign.

> One girl remembers the mortifying way her father tried to build up her strength against adversity. It was the first few months of high school. She was new to the school, new to town and very shy. Her father drove her to the busy front entrance of the school in his big black Cadillac, pounding on the horn all the way and laughing as the students passing by craned their necks to see what the racket was about. She would crouch down under the car seat, pleading with her father to stop. When she arrived at the school, instead of feeling stronger, she fled to the washroom to hide.

Dad's intentions were good. His timing was lousy. Between the ages of 13 and 14, children are incredibly self-conscious. Running them through the wringer won't wash out the wimpiness. There are more empathic approaches to toughen up a child.

If you have a temperamentally anxious child, give him the opportunity to try new things, coaching and encouraging him along the way. Even tickling—within reason—can raise a child's level of tolerance to adversity. Better yet, start from the minute your child is born to build his strength of character so that he has strong enough self-esteem not to bow to the bully's blows or to bully others himself.

BUILDING A PRE-SCHOOLER'S ASSERTIVENESS AND SELF-ESTEEM

> *Little Ryan has locked himself in the car again. He doesn't want to play with Tyler and nobody, nobody, can make him. It's so frustrating, his mother says. Ryan and Tyler used to be such good friends, just like their mothers. But early in toddlerhood their easy companionship soured. Like many two-year-olds, Tyler hit a lot. At age three, when the other kids started playing cooperatively, Tyler continued to be rough, hitting, kicking, even pushing Ryan down the stairs. When his parents rebuked him, he sulked in the corner until they felt guilty and apologized.*
>
> *Now at the age of five, the friendship has fizzled. Ryan refuses to get out of the car when his mother tries to visit her friend. When Tyler comes over to his house, Ryan runs up to his room to hide. "It's embarrassing," Ryan's mom says. "My son's wondering what's wrong with him and I've got to the point of hating this kid."*

It was apparent early on that little Tyler was going to be a handful. Without direction, limits or parents with backbone, he was a little bully-in-training. It's not unusual to see definite personality traits in children so young. Most parents and day-care workers can point out one or two boisterous children in a play group who seem, from day one, to be toddling directly towards trouble. And they can probably point out the tykes at the bottom of the toddler totem pole who seem destined to remain there, victims forever.

The former seem to be a little louder, rougher and a little less sensitive; the latter may cry more easily, seek shelter more readily. Obviously something has happened already in the short time these youngsters have been on earth to direct them to one side of the fence or the other. It has a lot to do with self-esteem or the lack thereof. And it probably began in the diaper days.

Parents can start bolstering their child's self-esteem from the minute they are born. When a baby is very young, the job of his primary caregiver is to do everything possible to make things right and good for him. Life should be as pleasant as possible in these tender months. Self-worth is the priority now; discipline comes later.

A healthy baby has a sense of entitlement. She makes a noise. Mommy comes. She learns that she can make things happen and people will listen to her. A caregiver teaches the baby a great deal just in the way he or she responds to the baby's crying. Studies show that, at three months, those babies whose parents were more sensitive and more responsive were more secure at the age of one year, and at nursery school they were better able to handle their peers and teachers. These are children who have learned to ask for help when they need it and to handle things on their own when they don't.

But if a baby get inconsistent responses from her care-givers in her first year, she will not learn that the world is a reliable place in which she can want something and go after it. Already she will have learned that she is not worth other people's trouble. She will have learned distrust. She will have learned to enter life with her fists up, looking for a fight—or she will have learned not to bother fighting at all.

In toddlerhood, the fireworks begin. Life is a rollicking

roller coaster of emotions. Hold on tight and ride it out. Enjoy it, if you can, with the knowledge that your child is growing up. If your toddler doesn't want to go to bed and makes no bones about telling you—good! You want your toddler to express his feelings with confidence.

But not with disrespect. If you don't like his tone of voice, say so. Watch your own tone of voice, too. If you yell, your child will think you are angry with him, rather than with the behavior. Yelling builds up the tension and makes some children even more contrary and aggressive, and possibly bullyish. When mom and dad are always reacting to his bad behavior, then grown-ups adopt the victim role, while the child becomes the bully at the helm. It may be better to try a more pro-active approach, like the popular 1-2-3 Magic program, developed by U.S. psychologist Dr. Thomas Phelan. It weeds through the weedling, whining and "why's?," giving preschoolers simple expectations instead. If the child is behaving in an unacceptable way, the caregiver tells him to stop, then begins counting in five-second intervals. If he has not stopped by the count of three a time-out is imposed.

When the waters are stormy, parents should provide these calm, consistent limits without guilt and realize that protests are inevitable. Frustrating as it may be, dealing with the protests is worth the time. Remember that this, too, will end. Brace yourself and tell yourself, "My child is strengthening himself for life." It can be a sort of mantra for your worst days of rebellion. Non-compliance is an important part of a child's development. It's a way to build assertiveness and acquire social skills that will help him when he's face-to-face with a bully.

TEACHING CHILDREN TO HANDLE ANGER
AND AGGRESSION

As toddlers, most kids begin to show some aggression. This is a crucial time for teaching what is appropriate and inappropriate behavior, before a child's self-image and roles are fully developed. Leaving two-year-olds to fend for themselves socially won't work. At this age, children don't understand the complexities of social behavior; it doesn't make sense to coerce two-year-olds to play cooperatively. In her egocentric mind she says, "I am the world and the world's here for me and I'd rather tear her hair out than let her touch my Barney doll!" Don't expect true cooperative play to happen until age four.

Toddlers and two-year-olds need lots of adult support, supervision and direction in basic assertiveness training. Billy wants Timmy's ball. He grabs it. Timmy cries. Both kids need a lesson before patterns are set. The aggressor needs a clear message that this is not acceptable behavior and there are alternatives: to ask, take turns, trade or borrow. If that strategy doesn't work, help him find a substitute for the toy. Console him, saying, "I know how you feel" and offer comfort instead of the ball. The idea is to teach him that acting frustrated and upset will not get him what he wants. Children need to learn how to live with being told "No."

Sometimes toddler aggression is really dangerous—when Tyler pushed Ryan down the stairs, for example. As a parent, there's a temptation to fly off the handle, whisk the offender away and punish him soundly. But that may only worsen the situation; physical interference will only infuriate the child. And toddlers learn by imitation. Don't spank or hit back.

Lectures on aggression won't help at this age either.

That doesn't mean you should ignore the aggression. The problem won't go away on its own. By saying nothing, the aggressor and all the kids who are witnessing the incident learn that bullying is acceptable. Instead, adults need to react quickly, clearly, calmly and tactfully. The victim should be comforted first, then the aggressor should be told that what he has done is not acceptable. Don't yell. Point out that his friend/victim is crying. Tell him that it's not okay to hurt people. Inform him that you don't want him to hurt anyone any more.

Even if he can't understand what you're saying, he'll get the message through your expression and tone of voice that he has done something wrong. Then use time out: separate the aggressor from the activity and let him know he is to stay away until he can play nicely. After a couple of minutes, get him involved in something else. Distraction may be the best forgiver of all.

But if the aggression doesn't stop, if he continues to struggle for that coveted toy, you've got to step in and you can't be wishy-washy about it. Experts suggest you remove the aggressor from the play group and tell him he can try to behave more gently next time. Follow through. Pack up your bags and go home.

He may have a temper-tantrum. That's normal too. Take it calmly and repeat your mantra to yourself: "My child is strengthening himself for life." Afterwards, be welcoming and caring and be reassured that your child is simply learning that he can't always get what he wants. A child who has learned this fact of life is less likely to bully others.

In any such conflict there should be a lesson for the victim too. He should be offered comfort, of course, but he shouldn't be overwhelmed with it. You don't want him to decide he likes being a victim because then the grownups shower him with attention. He also needs to be encouraged and supported to speak up. Ask him, "How does that make you feel? Do you like it when he does that? You need to tell him." Then show him how to say a strong "No!" Practice it. Encourage him to say, "That hurt my feelings. I'm not going to let you do that." If you can't tell who is the aggressor and who is the victim, it's best to give a quick lesson to both—"This kind of behavior is not allowed"—and distract them from the source of the problem. Trying to sort out who did what to whom is not a good idea.

In these early years, behavior that resembles bullying is common. Children are terribly egocentric and lack the ability to put themselves in someone else's place. It's not really bullying, but it can be bully training if it's not handled correctly.

Three- and four-year-olds don't yet have the maturity to deal with large groups of friends. They're learning social skills and a lot of other children are sometimes too much to handle; they're better behaved one-on-one. It's not unusual to find two preschoolers excluding a third from play or throwing mean comments at him. It's not because they want to be mean; they're just in over their heads and treading water as best they can.

That doesn't mean you should ignore the behavior though. The child who is being treated unkindly should be coached to say, "You hurt my feelings. If you keep doing that, I won't play with you." In private (where she won't be embarrassed), tell the child who has been mean that her behavior made her friend unhappy. Then try to keep play time one-on-one until your preschooler seems mature enough to handle more.

When children are older, around kindergarten age, the egocentricity of early childhood should have disappeared and you can start helping your child to appreciate another's point of view. By the time they are in school, children are more able to recognize and accept the rights of others along with differences in gender or color.

And by the time a child is eight or nine, he may finally be capable of putting himself in another's shoes. That's when you should expect your child to empathize with others and imagine what other people feel like.

Anger, too, can be a difficult emotion for little ones to deal with. You can help toddlers by letting them know that *feeling* anger is okay. What's not okay is *hurting* someone in anger. And remember, the best teacher is your example. Handle your own anger well and chances are good your children will do the same.

For the toddler who is especially volatile and emotional, tending to throw things in anger or frustration, try to teach him to put words to his feelings: "Are you angry because you can't get your train to work?" Eventually he'll get the hang of it, learning to verbalize and express himself clearly and safely.

Sometimes the unkind behavior of a three- or four-year-old comes not from meanness but from poorly expressed anger. An insult or teasing may be the only way he knows of venting strong feelings. Preschoolers should be allowed to feel anger, but they need help understanding their emotions and expressing them more clearly. After an unpleasant episode, when feelings have cooled off and you've got time alone with the perpetrator, point out in an unjudgmental way that he seems to have been angry with his friend and help him think of better ways he could have expressed that anger.

You should continue to show children how to cope with anger in healthier ways as they get older. Have them punch a pillow or draw an angry-looking picture, for example. The Grace Contrino Abrams Peace Education Foundation in Florida has some suggestions for children:

- Take time out: count to ten.
- Write a "mad note," describing how angry you are. Then rip the note into a million pieces.
- Postpone the conflict. Say, "I'm so mad I can't talk about it now. I'll phone you later."

HELPING CHILDREN DEAL WITH REJECTION

Blair hovers just outside the circle of boys at recess time. Suddenly one of the boys takes a flying leap at him and throws him to the ground. Casually the bully returns to his group. Blair slowly picks himself up and moves back toward the boys again. Another boy sticks his arm out and pushes Blair's head back roughly. A second child joins him, trips Blair back down to the ground again. Then they turn their backs on their victim and rejoin the group. But bruised little Blair doesn't give up; he returns to lurk near the boys some more. He seems to be performing a kind of desperate dance, badly wanting to be part of the group but being roughly rejected again and again. Next recess, he will still be on the outside, trying to join in, receiving beatings instead of friendship.

Some children just can't cope with rejection. They are so troubled by being excluded that they put up with being bullied in order to belong somewhere. They accept the abuse because they need contact so badly.

The way to avoid rejection problems is to teach children, when they are very young, how to accept rejection as a simple fact of life. It can start with small everyday battles, like the toddler who doesn't want daddy to go to work on Monday after a fun weekend. Reconcile him by saying, "Yes, it was a nice time with daddy. I wish he could stay here too. But you can play with him tonight." Then get on with your day confidently.

When an older child complains that Susan won't play with her, respond in the same empathetic, matter-of-fact way. "Yes, that's tough when someone doesn't want to play with you," you could say. Then explain that Susan has some troubles (if rejection by this child is chronic) or that she is probably in a bad mood and your child could try again another day. Then provide something else to do instead. When children reach the middle childhood years—seven to 11—it's time to move from bruised elbows to bruised egos. Dealing with rejection is one of their jobs in the less sheltered world they are entering. When your child comes home upset about a minor exclusion, make a neutral comment or question—"You seem bothered by something," and wait until she's ready to talk. Role-play to work out better responses, but don't obsess over the experience. Move on to some more positive aspects of her life. A child must learn that it's not the end of the world to be rejected; it may be a tough experience but it doesn't mean she's worthless.

FOSTERING INDEPENDENCE AND SOCIABILITY

Some children are more clingy than others. If your two-year-old child visits a play group and sticks by your side for a while before venturing away from you, don't worry. He's just displaying normal wariness and caution. It may take some children eight to ten visits before they are at ease enough to explore a social setting on their own. If that describes your child, accept it as part of his temperament. Don't push him away from you too soon or he will get the message that you're uncomfortable with his pace and may anxiously cling to you all the more.

What is more worrying, experts say, is a toddler who is socially indiscriminate. Children *should* exhibit a certain amount of pickiness. That's why it's bad to force physical affection on a child. If Sally doesn't want to give nice old Aunt Bea a kiss, be happy she is asserting her independence. If you force the issue, you run the risk of submerging her own impulses and body boundaries. It may be a good idea to talk to your child after she has asserted herself and tell her, "I like the way you stood up for yourself and your body limits." You can teach her to assert

---

WARNING SIGNS THAT A CHILD LACKS ASSERTIVENESS

- Excessive clinging—much more than other girls or boys of the same age
- School avoidance
- Not playing with friends
- Crying easily
- Withdrawal from the social world

If your child exhibits these traits, watch him in different situations. His behavior may be different at home than it is at school; he may be controlled and inhibited at school, but fine with the neighbors. If that's the case, you needn't worry. If you think your child lacks assertiveness, check your diagnosis first, not with his dad or grandma and grandpa but with an unbiased, trained observer. A teacher or day-care worker who has experience and has observed many children will know what is unusual or problematic.

herself without being rude, but never force her to do something with her body that she doesn't want.

Parents can also have a strong, behind-the-scenes effect on their child's social abilities. By subtly guiding your child, you can help him create his own network of friends and further strengthen his self-esteem. This is easier in the preschool years, when grownups are not yet outsiders. At this stage, you can choose their friends for them, stay close to the play area and teach them the art of negotiation. This is your time to coach and it may be your best chance to build a firm foundation for friendships to come.

When children get older you will have to step out of the picture somewhat. You can still offer guidance, however, even though you'll have to sleuth a bit to find out what's really going on. Talk with your children about school, but don't simply say, "What did you learn today?" Instead, ask what games were played at recess, how the games were played and listen between the lines.

Let your child know that you value his friendships, but if your child doesn't have many friends and still seems happy, don't worry about it. Child psychologists say some kids simply enjoy being on their own, just as some adults do, and we should respect their right to play independently. Keep in mind, however, that friendship can be a wonderful buffer. Studies show children with several friends are less likely to have discipline problems in school, possibly because having few friends may indicate difficulty getting along with others in general.

Reggie was a good student, great grades, no discipline problems, beautiful smile and gentle demeanor. He also loved computers and from the age of nine, he immersed himself in them. His parents encouraged it, assuming it would help him. They didn't notice how much time he was spending on-line, playing video games and putzing about. They didn't notice how often he opted for the computer instead of playing with friends. They didn't notice any of this until their son committed suicide.

Make sure there are plenty of opportunities to make friends and play with other children. Get her involved in extra-curricular activities. Structured lessons aren't the best place to build social skills since interaction is usually minimal. Play groups or outings are better. Let her take her time, watching and getting comfortable first. You can't push a child to be sociable.

To ease the way for a shy young child trying to fit into a play group, try this: at play time, when there are other children around, sit down with your child at an inviting-looking activity or craft. The other kids will probably slip in. Then you can bow out quietly. If a disagreement erupts in this tentative new friendship circle, help them to negotiate their way through it, letting them know that a disagreement isn't the end of a friendship.

Gary Ladd, a psychologist with the University of Illinois, says parents of children who are having trouble making—or keeping—friends should be aware of some possible problems. One common problem with unlikeable kids, he says, is that they approach play-time with self-centered agendas, concerned with how they can get their own way. They may engage in unfair turn-taking, greediness and ignoring others' feelings. These children may have been raised in overly permissive or indulgent households and taught a philosophy of "looking out for number one." Other unpopular kids may be disruptive, hyperactive, aggressive and blind to the fact that they are disliked by peers. These children may have been raised by emotionally rejecting and overly punitive parents. All of this points to the importance of parents' teaching kids social skills, kindness and fair play, at an early age.

Another reason to care about our children's friendships: Making and keeping friends is linked to academic success. "Regardless of how prepared children are academically, they still have to attach or engage themselves within the school environment," Ladd says. "And the glue that helps kids attach or engage—with young kids, four and five years old—is sometimes more interpersonal or social than it is academic."

Play games with your children. It is through games that children learn about rules for social behavior. By taking part in games with your kids you can model the kind of behavior that they need to learn to get along with their peers.

Sports activities are great, not only for building friendships but also for giving you at least a few hours each week during which you know where your child is and who she is with. At the same time, she is becoming more confident because she is developing skills she can be proud of.

Because friends are such strong influences on children's behavior, it pays to teach your child how to be his own peer police. Remind him to pay attention to his feelings when he is with friends. If he feels good about himself and what he is doing with them, then that's great. If not, it may be time to take a step back and reevaluate that friendship.

This self-monitoring can start at a young age. After play dates get him to ask himself, "Did we have fun together? Did we share/fight/laugh/cry? Was I happy? Was I bored?

If your child is bothered by something in a play date, encourage her to think of some ways to solve it. Reassure her that if she doesn't feel good about playing with a friend and she has tried unsuccessfully to make it better, then it's okay to walk away.

It's also a good idea to encourage your young child to speak up for herself. Too often we run to the rescue when we should be letting her use her own voice. If you are with a group of adults and are discussing your child, don't ignore her—welcome her input. Let her answer questions about herself rather than answering for her. In a store, if she wants to find a product or determine a price, let her ask the salesperson herself.

Older children assert their independence through bargaining, offering reasons why they don't want to obey your orders and searching for a compromise. This can be as frustrating and time-consuming for a parent as a toddler incessantly saying "No." But building negotiating skills is very important in developing social competence and it's worth the trouble. Tell yourself again, "My child is strengthening herself for life." Those same persuasive techniques she uses on you to get out of making her bed may one day be used to get out of a bout with a bully. Keep the lines of communication open every chance you get: in the car, switch off the radio and talk about the day. Eat dinner together without the telephone or television as distractions. (TV-Free America reports that 66 per cent of Americans regularly eat dinner while watching TV.) Use the few minutes just before bedtime for talk-time. One parent has their child talk about "one thing happy, one thing sad, one thing funny, one thing mad." It opens the door to all kinds of discussions. Instead of cramming your family calendar with individual pursuits and skills enrichment, try leaving some down-time for emotionally enriching experiences.

Encourage your child to talk about the full range of emotions and to learn words to express disappointment, frustration or tiredness. If you can be clear about how you feel, psychologists say, then you can be clear about what you need from others or how you want to be treated. A child who can get what he wants by expressing his needs verbally will come to see himself as effective and able to solve his own problems, not afraid of conflict and strong emotions, not afraid of the big bad bully.

TIPS FOR BUILDING STRENGTH

> *A group of bored 11- and 12-year-olds, unchallenged and understimulated, have come up with something exciting to do. Jimmy, who always seems on the edge of this cool group, trying desperately to squirm in, follows along. It turns out they're going elevator-hopping in a nearby apartment building. It's a dangerous activity— riding atop an elevator car—that has killed many children. When Jimmy balks at the idea, the cool dudes try with name-calling to twist his arm. Calling a boy "chicken" is like pressing a button when his self-esteem is low. Here's a chance to prove himself! Jimmy clambers aboard the rickety elevator roof and begins his descent.*

This is not the way to learn about risks and failure and getting along with others. A child with strong self-esteem knows that. That child is less likely to bow to bullying and less eager to climb aboard the elevator and put himself and his future in jeopardy.

Low self-esteem is like an open door to bullies. Parents can slam it shut with a few smart moves in a child's developing years. Experts suggest the following:

- Help your child to think daily of things he did that made him feel proud. Having self-confidence in one area enables him to face difficulties in another.
- Remind him that it's okay to make mistakes. Provide controlled risks so that your child can build up his courage safely and learn not to be devastated by failure. In fact, let him make a few mistakes and show him how to deal with it. If your preschooler wants to ride his big brother's two-wheeler, for example, let him give it a shot—just be sure you're there to kiss the skinned knees when he falls and to put him back in the saddle again.
- Teach him how to correct negative thoughts and turn them into positive ones: not "I can't do that puzzle, I'm dumb" but rather "This puzzle is tough, but I can do it. I'll try again or I'll ask for help."
- Encourage your child to accept tough challenges by emphasizing that trying is the goal—not necessarily succeeding. If he wants to try out for the rep team in hockey and hasn't a hope in hell of making it, let him, reminding him that he is doing it to learn how to perform under pressure, how to handle try-outs in general.
- Acknowledge your child's needs but at the same time provide consistent and firm discipline.
- When discipline is necessary, don't humiliate or malign the child. Instead, focus on the behavior. If Michael is late coming home for dinner, the wrong response is: "I've told you countless times not to be

late. What's the matter with you? Can't you remember anything?" The right response spells the problem out in terms of consequences. "I told you this morning it's important that we have dinner together. Now you're going to be late for practice."

- Spend quality time with your child. Point out his strengths and talents to make him feel well-loved and important.

- Praise your child for working hard on a problem rather than for being smart or good at something. This will help him view difficulties as surmountable and not a result of some skill or talent he lacks.

- Teach your child not to give up his possessions too readily. If toys are being taken from him, help him to practice saying "I'm using this right now."

- A very tight, authoritarian upbringing can cause a child to draw into a shell. Encourage him to talk about his feelings and thoughts at an early age and to speak up about his needs. Let him vent. Don't admonish him when he tells you he hates Jimmy. Draw him out so that he discovers with his own words other ways of expressing anger. In family discussions, give him an opportunity to provide his own feedback, so that he feels important and heard.

- Set limits. Kids need to know how much candy they can eat or how late to stay out. Limits must be fair and consistent and should be set with adequate explanations.

- Determine appropriate roles for the child and parent. This is especially important with single parents, who sometimes confide everything in their children. These children often end up feeling responsible for solving problems and making their parents happy.

It's okay for a child to know a parent is having a hard time and is worrying, but he doesn't need to know all the details.

- Provide lots of healthy activities so a child is not tempted by boredom to do something stupid (like be bullied into doing something dangerous) or mean (like bullying others).

- When he makes a mistake, help him put it in perspective. Say, "That's too bad. Let's try again." Or, "When I made that very same mistake, I tried this ..." Laugh about your own mistakes, but never laugh at his.

SIBLINGS AND THE FAMILY BULLY

It is in the family that children explore the extremes of emotion. What parent hasn't glowed at the incredibly tender, deeply loving and protective way their children can be with each other? What parent hasn't been floored by the hostility, jealousy and anger that can explode between siblings in the blink of an eye?

The principal characteristic of sisters and brothers is their permanence. If a family member bugs you, you can't say, "I won't be your sibling any more." As a result, everyone feels a little more free with their emotions and behavior.

And brothers and sisters are conveniently available. If you're dealing with feelings of hostility, you can't take it out on your parents as easily as you can on your sibling. There is also an important, inherent power differential. Unless children are twins, someone is always younger or older, bigger or smaller. That's why sibling relationships can be so powerful in teaching lessons about aggression. And that's why it's extremely important for parents to be watchful.

Sibling warfare worries us and rightly so. A brother

who makes constant, subtle, snide remarks can whittle away at his sibling's self-esteem. And a sister who sneers at her sibling's achievements can leave scars that last a lifetime. Bullying starts here, and parents must protect their children to ensure the power struggle doesn't set unhealthy patterns of bullying and victimization.

Parents need to provide empathetic intervention—understanding each child and the developmental stage he's at—when children are very young. It's not realistic to expect preschool children to work out their conflicts. Your timely intervention will teach them how to handle differences so that when children get older—sometime between the ages of six to nine—they will be able to deal with most conflicts on their own.

And don't worry if, during those early years, you find yourself stepping in frequently. If a one-year-old who worships her three-year-old brother decides to "help" with his building blocks, a parent needs to handle this, allowing the younger child the capacity for exploration and a link with her brother at the same time as protecting the older child's castle and helping him cope with feelings of hostility.

If the elder child is left alone and hurts the younger, she will feel guilty and may do more; not able to bear the guilt, she may hurt him again to reassure herself that it doesn't really bother him. Young children don't yet have inner control, experts say, and they can get quite disturbed by the consequences of their own aggression.

But parents need to know when to stay out too. Siblings should realize that it's okay to have negative feelings for each other sometimes. If you insist that everything be wonderful all the time, you can count on it not being so. Let your children vent their angry feelings by talking, drawing pictures, using play dough or digging holes in the sand—whatever it takes to blow off steam.

Put-downs and insults that can cause deep damage should never be allowed, but don't take sides in a sibling squabble. By identifying the victim and the bully in a dispute, you may be reinforcing roles that children feel bound to follow. Besides, it's tough to know exactly who the bully is. Many adults remember a younger sibling who was great at getting sympathy with crocodile tears—and pinches on the sly.

It may help to explain what either child is feeling. Describe their emotions: "Jimmy, you're angry that Laura wants to play with her friends instead of you right now," or "Laura, you're frustrated because, although you enjoy Jimmy's company, you sometimes want to be on your own." This will help defuse feelings and let each child know that you understand what they're going through. It will give them a feeling of respect and make them more open to cooperating on a solution.

If you practice healthy parental intervention when your kids are young, then when a seven-year-old comes complaining to you about the ten-year-old, you can feel more confident in sending them off to work it out on their own, though you should still have a good sense of what's happening. You have gradually taken away your support and left them with the tools to solve their conflicts themselves.

Older children can have fun cooking up solutions to their squabbles. And if it's their solution, they may be more likely to live with it. If they can't figure out a solution, guide them. These are great teachable moments in which kids can learn about conflict resolution, self-expression and assertiveness.

HELPING YOUR CHILD TO HELP OTHERS

"I was a typical child who stood by and did nothing except feel horrified as I watched other helpless children terrorized," says Margaret, recalling her school days. *"I remember a kid in my Grade 3 class who was hounded mercilessly, overlooked in group activities and even brutalized. What was his defect? He was overweight and had red hair. It seems so trivial, but it was enough to make him the target of so much teasing and brutality that I am sure it affects him today. I admit I still feel guilty that I didn't stand up for him then, but there was so much peer pressure to remain silent at least, if not join in on the fun, that I found it impossible to help him. His name was Tommy. To all the Tommys out there, I wish I could say, 'It wasn't your fault. And I'm so sorry.'"*

The pressure to conform, to keep mum, as Margaret did, is incredibly intense for children. That pressure has a pretty good hold on grownups too. When you think about the number of adults who won't get involved when they hear a stranger's screams, it shouldn't surprise us that children are any different. But that old saying "If you're not part of the solution you're part of the problem" was never more true than in a bullying episode. By silently watching a bully cause trouble or, worse yet, laughing at his jokes, children are giving their approval and egging him on.

Unfortunately, most children feel helpless and disturbed in the presence of a bully. Research shows that most children dislike bullying, find it a major concern and would like to help stop it. But quite often they simply can't. The peer pressure that surrounds a bully is overpowering. Those who do muster up enough courage to try to help the victim are usually lone voices in the wilderness. Pint-sized witnesses often can't help but be sucked into the bully's maelstrom of persecution.

But there are things parents can do to encourage the kind of brave, good citizenship that is required of children who witness bullying and want it to stop.

Ask your child, "What is a bully?" Ask her what other children do to help stop bullying. Ask her what might stop a bully from tormenting or excluding another child. This way you'll raise the idea that there are other ways of handling a school bully and that she can play a part.

When you hear of a bullying episode at your child's school, use it as an opportunity to discuss playground dynamics. Talk to him about how he can be subconsciously drawn into peer pressure. If you learn he giggled along with the teasing, ask him, "What did you think you were doing by laughing—being the friend of a strong person or not being bullied?"

Emphasize that by their silence they are contributing to the problem. Tell them that in the future, their smartest move might be to tell a teacher or another adult. You could also encourage them to befriend the bullied child and be kind to the bully when he is *not* being a bully.

Encourage your child to care for others, beginning with early lessons in sharing and telling the truth, moving on to caring for the family pet or younger siblings, then helping out at the local food bank, collecting for UNICEF at Halloween or giving away old toys.

It can be especially meaningful for children to help other children. One neat new program based in Las

Gatos, California, for example, arranges for children to play with other kids at homeless shelters, visit the chronically ill and those with special needs and tutor academically challenged kids (see Kids Cheering Kids in the Resources section). Studies show children with experience helping others have greater independence and self-confidence. And if they learn early to speak out and take a stand, they may be less inclined to watch a bully incident in silence.

Parents should demonstrate empathy for others, making the quality conspicuous enough that children can observe and learn. If you see another child fall and hurt himself in the park, for example, go to him and help, making sure your child sees what you're doing. Describe the motivation behind your actions: "Oh, he's crying, he must be hurt. He's holding his leg. That must hurt. Let's see if we can help." And above all, show good citizenship yourself. Speak out about injustice and encourage your child to do so too.

> *"It really, really bothers me that Stuart sees the world as a rosy place where everything's good and fun,"* says one father of his two-year-old boy, a child who already shows signs of being small and shy. *"I know that some day some son-of-a-bitch kid is going to try to make him feel like dirt. I don't want that to happen to him. It just isn't fair."*

It can be a scary thing for parents to look down the rocky path their children must hike during their childhood years: at the journey his daughter must travel alone, at the not-so-nice strangers and classmates her son will meet along the way. You can't go there for them and you can't face those foes for them. But you can prepare them for the battles to come. By laying the groundwork and a firm foundation of love and self-esteem, you can teach your children how to be assertive in this aggressive world.

Endnotes

Complete bibliographical information on the sources cited below is provided in the Bibliography.

CHAPTER 1—THE NATURE OF BULLYING
[1] David P. Farrington, "Understanding and Preventing Bullying" (1993). This is part of a long-term study that followed approximately 400 London boys through their childhood years, interviewing them eight times from the time they were eight years old until they were 32 years old.

CHAPTER 2—UNDERSTANDING THE BULLY
[1] Suzanne Ziegler (Board of Education, City of Toronto), Alice Charach (C. M. Hincks Research Institute, Toronto) and Debra Pepler (York University), *Bullying at School* (1993), p. 8. The same survey showed 20 per cent of students had been bullied more than once or twice, and 8 per cent were bullied weekly or more often.

[2] Alan J.C. King and Beverly Coles, *The Health of Canada's Youth: Views and Behaviours of 11-, 13-, and 15-year-olds from 11 Different Countries* (1992), p. 65. The United States was not included in this survey, but observers say the prevalence of bullying south of the border is similar, if not higher.

[2a] Christine S. Asidao, Shontelle Vion, Dorothy L. Espelage, "Interviews with Middle School Students: Bullying, Victimization and Contextual Factors," *Journal of Early Adolescence* (1999).

[2b] From an interview-based study by Asidao, Vion and Espelage (1999).

[3] "Student Victimization at School," U.S. Department of Education, National Center for Educational Statistics, National Household Education Survey (1995).

[4] Wendy Craig, Ray Peters and Roman Konarski, *The National Longitudinal Survey of Children and Youth*, Human Resources and Development Canada (1998).

[5] Diana L. Paulk, Ed.S., Susan M. Swearer, Ph.D., Sam Song, M.Ed., Paulette Tam Carey, M.A., Unversity of Nebraska-Lincoln. "Teacher-, Peer-, and Self-Nominations of Bullies and Victims of Bullying."

[6] Debra Pepler et al., "Aggression in the Peer Group: Assessing the Negative Socialization Process" (1993).

[7] C. Ryan, F. Mathews, and J. Banner, *Student Perceptions of Violence*. Toronto: Central Toronto Youth Services, 1993.

[8] R.E. Tremblay et al., "Violent Boys: Development and Prevention" (Forum on Corrections Research, 1991), pp. 29–35.

[9] David P. Farrington, "Understanding and Preventing Bullying" (1993).

[10] I. Whitney and P. K. Smith, "A Survey of the Nature

and Extent of Bullying in Junior/Middle and Secondary Schools," *Educational Research*, 35 (1), Spring (1993).

[11] Wendy M. Craig, Debra J. Pepler and Jennifer Connolly, "Bullying: High School Analysis of Form Context Mediators and Consequences" (1998).

[12] Craig, Peters and Konarski, *National Longitude Survey*.

[13] Andrew Mellor, *Bullying in Scottish Secondary Schools* (1990).

[14] Fred Mathews, "Youth Gangs on Youth Gangs," Central Toronto Youth Services, Solicitor General Canada (1988), p. 25.

[15] Wendy M. Craig and Debra J. Pepler, *Contextual Factors in Bullying and Victimization* (1992).

[16] Suzanne Ziegler et al., *Bullying at School* (1993), p. 11.

[17] Mathews, "Youth Gangs on Youth Gangs," p. 32.

[18] CNN, October 1998.

[19] National Crime Prevention Council, Washington, D.C.

[20] Barbara Dafoe Whitehead, "Dan Quayle Was Right" (*Atlantic Monthly*, April 1993), p. 77.

CHAPTER 4—UNDERSTANDING THE VICTIM

[1] Ziegler and Rosenstein-Manner, *Bullying at School: Toronto in an International Context*, August 1991, p. 22.

[2] Stephen Nowicki Jr. and Marshall P. Duke, *Helping the Child Who Doesn't Fit In* (1992).

[3] G. W. Ladd, S. H. Birch, and E. Buhs. (2000). "Children's social and scholastic lives in kindergarten: Related spheres of influence?" *Child Development*.

Ladd, G. W. & Kochenderfer, B. J. (1998). Parenting behaviors and the parent-child relationship: Correlates of peer victimization in kindergarten? *Developmental Psychology*, 34,1450–1458.

Ladd, G. W. & Kochenderfer, B. J. & Coleman, C. C. (1997). Classroom peer acceptance, friendship, and victimization: Distinct relational systems that contribute uniquely to children's school adjustment? *Child Development*, 68, 1181–1197.

Kochenderfer, B. J. & Ladd, G. W. (1996). "Peer victimization: Cause or consequence of school maladjustment?" *Child Development*, 67, 1305–1317.

Ladd, G. W. (1996). Shifting ecologies during the 5–7 year period: Predicting children's adjustment during the transition to grade school. In A. Sameroff & M. Haith (Eds.) *The Five to Seven Year Shift* (pp. 363–386). Chicago, IL: University of Chicago Press.

Kochenderfer, B. J., & Ladd, G. W. (1997). Victimized children's responses to peers' aggression: Behaviors associated with reduced versus continued victimization. *Development and Psychopathology*, 9, 59–73.

[4] Lisa A. Serbin et al.,"Childhood Aggression and Withdrawal as Predictors of Adolescent Pregnancy, Early Parenthood, and Environmental Risk for the Next Generation" (1991).

[5] Suzanne Ziegler et al., *Bullying at School* (1993), p. 12. This study found that 30 per cent of victims reported that neither their teachers nor their parents had talked to them about being bullied. When a group of elementary school children were asked about whether they sought adult help when they were being bullied, 47 per cent of victims indicated that they had told their teachers, 63 percent indicated that they had told their parents, but 28 percent of victims indicated that they had told neither their teachers nor their parents.

[6] Ibid, p. 8.

CHAPTER 5—HELPING THE VICTIM: THE PARENTS' ROLE

[1] Alan J.C. King and Beverly Coles, The Health of Canada's Youth (1992), p. 65.

[2] Andrew Mellor, The Scottish Council for Research in Education (1990).

[3] For more information, see the section on Resource Groups.

[4] According to Metro Toronto Police, 93 per cent of the time the victim's weapon is used on the victim.

CHAPTER 6—HELPING THE VICTIM: THE SCHOOL'S ROLE

[1] Alan J.C. King and M.J. Peart, *Teachers in Canada: Their Work and Quality of Life* (1992). This was a national study for the Canadian Teachers' Federation, Social Program Evaluation Group.

[2] Barbara Dafoe Whitehead, "Dan Quayle Was Right" (*Atlantic Monthly*, April 1993), p. 77.

[3] Wendy M. Craig and Debra J. Pepler, "Observations of Bullying and Victimization on the Schoolyard," *Canadian Journal of School Psychology* (1997).

[4] Wendy M. Craig and Debra J. Pepler, *Contextual Factors in Bullying and Victimization* (1992), p. 8.

[5] Suzanne Ziegler and Merle Rosenstein-Manner, *Bullying at School: Toronto in an International Context* (1991).

[6] Ronald R. Dale, "Mixed Versus Single-Sex Schools: The Social Aspect of Bullying" (1991).

[7] David M. Day (Ontario Correctional Institute), Carol A. Golench (Ontario Institute for the Studies in Education/University of Toronto), "Promoting Safe Schools Through Policy: Results of a Survey of Canadian School Boards" (February 1997).

[8] Day and Golench, "Promoting Safe Schools."

CHAPTER 7—THE BULLY IN SOCIETY

[1] Stats are from TV-Free America, a non-profit group that encourages people to reduce TV-watching and raise awareness of its harmful effects. It also sponsors an annual National TV Turn-off Week. Organizers' kit available from:

TV-Free America
1322 18th Street N.W.
Washington, D.C. 20036

[2] David A. Walsh, "Video Game Violence: What Does the Research Say?" National Institute on Media and the Family (1998).

[3] N. Schutte, J. Malouff, J. Post-Gorden, and A. Rodasta, "Effects of Playing Video Games on Children's Aggressive and Other Behaviors," *Journal of Applied Social Psychology.* 1988, 18:454–460.

[4] S. Silvern and P. Williamson, "The Effects of Video Game Play on Young Children's Aggression, Fantasy, and Prosocial Behavior," *Journal of Applied Developmental Psychology.* 1987, 8:453–462; J. Cooper and D. Mackie, "Video Games and Aggression in Children," *Journal of Applied Social Psychology.* 1986, 16:726–744; A. Irwin and A. Gross, "Cognitive Tempo, Violent Video Games, and Aggressive Behavior in Young Boys," *Journal of Family Violence.* 1995, 10:337–350.

[5] S. Kirsh, "Seeing the World Through Mortal Kombat-Colored Glasses: Violent Video Games and the Development of a Short-Term Hostile Attribution Bias," *Childhood: A Global Journal of Child Research.* 1998, 5:177–184.

[6] Robert Abelman, *Some Children Under Some Conditions: TV and the High Potential Kid*, released by the National Research Center on the Gifted and Talented,

Cleveland State University in Ohio. The study, which includes a review of decades of research findings, cites research showing that gifted preschool kids typically watch two to three more hours of TV per week than do other children of the same age. They find TV an interesting and accessible source of information; it gives them an opportunity to observe and familiarize themselves with advanced or abstract concepts that are normally learned at a later age through other means, and it exposes them to complex themes and story lines at an earlier age. However, gifted children reduce their TV viewing sharply once they reach school age, and then watch less TV than their peers. The research found gifted kids are more likely to be involved in plot and story line, and less likely to be confused by TV programs. They are also less likely to be influenced by TV violence (which seems to have more impact on low achievers or naturally aggressive kids).

[7] Sandra Campbell, Federation of Women Teachers' Associations of Ontario newsletter, October/November 1992.

[8] L.D. Eron and L.R. Huesman, "The Role of Television in the Development of Pro-Social and Anti-Social Behaviour," *Development of Anti-Social and Pro-Social Behaviour*, Eds. D. Olweus, J.R. Block, M. Radke-Yarrow (N.Y. Academic Press, 1985), pp. 285–314.

[9] L.D. Eron, "The Problem of Media and Violence and Children's Behavior," Occasional Papers of the H.F. Guggenheim Foundation #7 (1993).

[10] National Institute on Media and the Family, National Survey of Family Media Habits.

[11] TV-Free America

[12] National Institute on Media and the Family National Survey of Family Media Habits, Knowledge and Attitudes (May 6, 1999).

Resource Groups

The Association of Parent Support Groups of Ontario, which provides support to parents whose kids have trouble with drugs, alcohol or discipline, is hoping to form a national association and has a list of similar support groups for parents across the country. For information write to APSGO, 4141 Twine Crescent, Mississauga, Ont. L4Z 1E4, or call the 24-hour help line: (416) 223-7444.

The Atrium Society offers conferences, teacher training, workshops, services and resources related to conflict resolution and peace education. 1-800-848-6021 or P.O. Box 816, Middlebury, Vermont, 05753.

Children's Creative Response to Conflict, Box 271, 523 North Broadway, Nyack, NY 10960, (914) 358-4601, offers workshops for families, teachers and children on conflict resolution and has a network of affiliate groups across the U.S.

The Grace Contrino Abrams Peace Education Foundation, 3550 Biscayne Boulevard, Suite 400, Miami, Florida 33137, (305) 576-5075, offers workshops, literature and audio- and videotapes on non-violent ways to resolve conflict.

Educators for Social Responsibility, 475 Riverside Drive, Room 450, New York, NY 10115.

The Martin Luther King, Jr. Center for Nonviolent Social Change, 449 Auburn Avenue, N.E. Atlanta, GA 30312, (404) 524-1956.

Men for Change—a Halifax-based group of men opposed to violence, which has developed a new violence-prevention junior high school curriculum, meets monthly to discuss what it is to be male in today's world. Box 3305, Quinpool Postal Outlet, Halifax, Nova Scotia B3L 4T6, or (902) 422-8476.

The National Coalition on Television Violence, Box 2157 Champaign, Illinois 61820, (217) 384-1920.

Parents for Youth is Toronto-based parents' support group to help parents who can't cope with out-of-control teenagers. It's run by a child-adolescent psychiatrist, Dr. Harvey Armstrong, on a fee-for-service basis. Call (416) 921-8092.

Save Our Sons and Daughters is an American grassroots organization based in Detroit, Michigan, which helps parents cope with and reduce violence among youth. It offers counselling for survivors of violence, violence-prevention programs and a peace curriculum for schools. Write to 2441 West Grand Boulevard, Detroit, Michigan 48208, (313) 361-5200.

Some cities offer assertiveness classes for children, such as the Child Assault Prevention Project provided by the Montreal Assault Prevention Centre, to help them ward off not just bullies but all attacks. For information on the Montreal project, call (514) 284-1212.

Some children with learning disabilities may find help in assertiveness training or social-skills classes such as those offered by some learning-disability associations. The associations also offer information for parents. Write to the Learning Disabilities Association of Canada, Chapel Street, Suite 200, Ottawa, Ont. K1N 7Z2, or call (613) 238-5721, or contact the Learning Disabilities Association of America, 4156 Library Road, Pittsburgh, PA 15234 (412) 341-1515.

RESOURCES

The Alliance for Children and Television
Prime Time Parent multi-media workshop kit
60 St. Clair Avenue East, Suite 1002
Toronto, Ontario
M4T 1N5
(416) 515-0466
(416) 515-0467 (fax)

Big Brothers Big Sisters of America
230 North 13th Street
Philadelphia, Pennsylvania 19107
(215) 567-7000
(215) 567-0394 (fax)
www.bbbsa.org

Bully B'ware Productions
1421 King Albert Avenue
Coquitlam, British Columbia
V3J 1Y3
www.bullybeware.com
(604) 936-8000
1-888-55BULLY

Evergreen Foundation
355 Adelaide Street West—Suite 5A
Toronto, Ontario
M5V 1S2
(416) 596-1495
(416) 596-1443 (fax)
www.evergreen.ca

International School Peace Gardens
3343 Masthead Crescent
Mississauga, Ontario
L5L 1G9
(905) 820-5067
(905) 820-6536 (fax)
www.geocities.com/RainForest/Vines/6016

Kids Cheering Kids
P.O. Box 2359
Las Gatos, California, 95031
1-888-KIDS-PLAY
(408) 353-2033
www.KidsCheeringKids.org

Kids Help Line
1-800-668-6868
http://kidshelp.sympatico.ca
(searching for numbers for childshelp.usa and boystown)

Media*Wise* Media*Quotient*
Resource kits for educators, parents and community
leaders
1-888-672-5437

National Association of School Psychologists
4340 East West Highway #402
Bethesda, Maryland 20814
(301) 657-0270

National Crime Prevention Council
1700 K Street, NW, Second Floor
Washington, DC 20006-3817
(202) 466-6272
(202) 296-1356 (fax)
www.weprevent.org

National Gardening Association
180 Flynn Avenue
Burlington, Vermont 05401
(802) 863-1308
(802) 863-5962 (fax)

National PTA
330 North Wabash Avenue, Suite 2100
Chicago, Illinois 60611
(312) 670-6782
www.pta.org

National School Safety Center
4165 Thousand Oaks Blvd, Ste 290
Westlake Village, California 91362
(805) 373-9977
(805) 373-9277 (fax)
www.nssc1.org

National Youth Gang Information Center
Institute for Intergovernmental Research
PO Box 12729
Tallahassee, Florida 33217
(850) 385-0600
(850) 386-5356 (fax)
www.iir.com/nygc/

Prime Mentors of Canada
(416) 923-6641 (ext. 2464)

Youth Crime Watch of America
9300 South Dadeland Blvd., Ste. 100
Miami, Florida 33156
(305) 670-2409
(305) 670-3805 (fax)
www.ycwa.org

Recommended Reading

RECOMMENDED READING FOR CHILDREN

To help children cope with shyness:

Feeling Left Out, by Kate Petty and Charlotte Firmin (Barron's, 1991)

Making Friends, by Kate Petty and Charlotte Firmin (Barron's, 1991)

Little Miss Shy, by Roger Hargreaves (Windermere, Florida: Rourke Enterprises Inc., 1981)

Shy Charles, by Rosemary Wells (New York: Dial Books for Young Readers, 1988)

What Mary Jo Shared, by Janice May Udry (Scholastic, 1991)

Stargone John, by Ellen Kindt McKenzie (Henry Holt, 1992)

Seven Days to a Brand-new Life, by Ellen Conford (Scholastic, 1993)

To help children build self-esteem and assertiveness:

Liking Myself, by Pat Palmer (Impact Publishers, 1977). Assertiveness training for children ages 5 to 9.

The Mouse, The Monster and Me! by Pat Palmer (Impact Publishers, 1977). Assertiveness concepts for 8 to 12-year-olds.

Stick Up for Yourself! Every Kid's Guide to Personal Power and Positive Self-Esteem, by Gershen Kaufman and Lev Raphael (Minneapolis: Free Spirit Publishing, 1990)

I Want It, by Elizabeth Crary, A Children's Problem-Solving Book (Parenting Press Inc., 1982)

Feelings, by Aliki (Mulberry Paperback Book, 1984)

Coping With Peer Pressure, by Leslie Kaplan (Rosen, 1989)

To help children deal with violence and bullying:

Move Over Twerp, by M. Alexander (Dial Books for Young Readers, E.P. Dutton, 1987).

No More Bullying, by Rosemary Stones (Dinosaur Publications, HarperCollins, 1991)

Bully on the Bus, by Carl W. Bosch, part of The Decision is Yours series (Parenting Press, 1988)

I Am Not a Crybaby, by Norma Simon and Helen Cogancherry (Niles, Illinois: A. Whitman, 1989)

Being Bullied, by Kate Petty and Charlotte Firmin (Barron's, 1991)

My Name Is Not Dummy, by Elizabeth Crary, A Children's Problem-Solving Book (Parenting Press Inc., 1983)

Why Is Everybody Picking on Me? A Guide to Handling Bullies For Young People, by Terrence Webster-Doyle (Atrium Society, Middlebury, Vermont, 1991)

A Kid's Guide to How to Stop the Violence, by Ruth Harris
Terrell (a Byron Press Book, an Avon Camelot Book, 1992)
Everything You Need to Know About: Street Gangs, by
Evan Stark (Rosen, 1992)
Coping With Street Gangs, by Margot Webb (Rosen, 1990)
So?, by Sheila White, City of North York Mayor's Office
(available through the North York Youth Group, 5330
Yonge Street, Suite 4, North York, Ontario M2N 5P9).
An anti-racism book for children.
68 Snappy Comebacks to Racist Jokes, by Sheila White,
City of North York Mayor's Office (see above)

For younger children:
Dealing with Bullying, by Marianne Johnston (Hazelden,
1998)
Tyrone the Double Dirty Rotten Cheater, by Hans
Wilhelm (Scholastic, 1991)
Bootsie Barker Bites, by Barbara Bottner (Putnam, 1992)
King of the Playground, by Phyllis Reynolds Naylor
(Macmillan, 1991)
School Isn't Fair, by Patricia Baehr (Macmillan, 1989)
Bully Trouble, by Joanna Cole (Random, 1989)
Tell Me Your Best Thing, by Anna Grossnickle Hines
(Dutton, 1991)
Joshua T. Bates Takes Charge, by Susan Shreve (Knopf,
1993)
Luke's Bully, by Elizabeth Winthrop (Viking, 1990)

For the middle years:
The Magic Book, by Willo Davis Roberts (Macmillan,
1986)
Dear God, Help!! Love, Earl, by Barbara Park (Knopf,
1993)

A Bundle of Sticks, by Pat Rhoads Mauser (Macmillan, 1987)

What a Wimp!, by Carol Carrick (Houghton, 1983)

Wendy and the Bullies, by Nancy K. Robinson (Scholastic, 1983)

Fight for Honor, by Carin G. Baker (Puffin, 1992)

Molly Maguire: Wide Receiver, by Ann Sullivan (Avon, 1992)

For the older child:

The Boy who Lost His Face, by Louis Sachar (Knopf, 1989)

Seventh Grade Weirdo, by Lee Wardlaw (Scholastic, 1992)

Hang On, Harvey!, by Nancy J. Hopper (Dell, 1994)

RECOMMENDED READING FOR PARENTS AND TEACHERS

Books dealing with self-esteem:

Peer-Pressure: A Parent-Child Manual, by Maria Sullivan (Tor Books, 1991)

I Think I Can, I Know I Can: Using Self-Talk to Help Raise Confident, Secure Kids, by Susan Isaacs and Wendy Ritchie (St. Martin's Press, 1989)

The Magic of Encouragement: Nurturing Your Child's Self-Esteem, by Stephanie Marston (New York: Morrow, 1990)

Smiling at Yourself: Educating Young Children About Stress and Self-Esteem, by Allen Mendler (E.T.R. Publishers, 1992)

Peer Pressure: How to Teach Young People to Be Assertive, Independent and Self-Confident, by Maria Sullivan (New York: Tom Doherty Associates, 1989)

Books for parents and teachers helping children with difficulties:

Helping the Child Who Doesn't Fit In, by Stephen Nowicki Jr. and Marshall P. Duke (Peachtree Publishers Ltd, 1992)

The Prepare Curriculum: Teaching Prosocial Competencies, by Arnold Goldstein (Research Press, 1988)

Skillstreaming in Early Childhood: Teaching Prosocial Skills to the Preschool and Kindergarten Child, by Ellen McGinnis and Arnold Goldstein (Research Press, 1990)

Skillstreaming the Adolescent: A Structured Learning Approach to Teaching Prosocial Skills, by Arnold Goldstein, Robert Sprafkin, Jane Gershaw, and Paul Klein (Research Press, 1980)

Skillstreaming the Elementary School Child: A Guide for Teaching Prosocial Skills, by Ellen McGinnis and Arnold Goldstein et al. (Research Press, 1984)

When Good Kids Do Bad Things: A Survival Guide for Parents, by Katherine G. Levine (New York: Norton, 1991)

When Kids Get Into Trouble, revised edition, by Priscilla Platt (Toronto: Stoddart, 1990)

The Difficult Child: Understanding and Managing Hard-to-Raise Children, by Stanley Turecki (Toronto: Bantam Books, 1985)

Boys Will Be Boys, by Myriam Miedzian (Doubleday, 1991)

Aggression Replacement Training: A Comprehensive Intervention for Aggressive Youth, by Arnold Goldstein and Barry Glick et al. (Research Press, 1987)

No One to Play With: The Social Side of Learning Disabilities, by Betty Osman (Academic Therapy, 1982)

Bullying: A Practical Guide to Coping for Schools, edited by Michele Elliott (Harlow: Longman, 1991)

Bullying at School: What We Know and What We Can Do,
by Dan Olweus (Blackwell Publishers, 1993)

For more ideas on healthy playground activities:

The Canadian Heart and Stroke Foundation offers a skipping games resource book. Call (416) 489-7100.

The Canadian Association for Health, Physical Education and Recreation has several resources for teachers through its Quality Daily Physical Education Project, including "K-3 Games" and "Fitness Fun." It also offers a Parents' Kit to help parents ensure quality phys-ed programming at their schools. Write 1600 James Naismith Dr., Gloucester, Ont. K1B 5N4.

The Canadian Intramural Recreation Association has developed a student leadership training package. Write 1600 James Naismith Dr., Gloucester, Ont. K1B 5N4.

The National Association for Sport and Physical Education also offers information about healthy games and recess activities. Write 1900 Association Drive, Reston, VA 22091, or call (703) 476-3410.

On raising children in difficult times:

Saving Childhood: Protecting our Children From the National Assault on Innocence, by Michael Medved and Diane Medved (New York: Harper Collins, 1998)

On Killing: The Psychological Cost of Learning to Kill in War and Society, by Lieutenant Colonel Dave Grossman, (Boston: Little Brown, 1995, 1996)

Nurturing Good Children Now: 10 Basic Skills to Protect and Strengthen Your Child's Core Self, by Ron Taffel with Melinda Blau (New York: Golden Books, 1999)

The Resilient Child: Preparing Today's Youth for Tomorrow's World, by Joanne M. Joseph (New York: Plenum Press, 1994)

On children with special needs:

"Why Doesn't Anybody Like Me?" A Guide to Raising Socially Confident Kids, by Hara Estroff Marano (New York: William Morrow, 1998)

Helping Your Anxious Child: An Effective Treatment for Childhood Fears, by David Lewis (London: Methuen, 1988)

Teaching Your Children Sensitivity, by Linda and Richard Eyre (New York: Simon & Schuster, 1987, 1995)

Parenting a Child with a Behavior Problem, by Penny Paquette and Cheryl Gerson Tuttle (Los Angeles: Lowell House, 1995, 1996)

On children and the media:

Getting Unplugged: Take control of Your Family's Television, Video Game and Computer Habits, by Joan Anderson and Robin Wilkins New York: John Wiley & Sons, 1998)

TV-Proof Your Kids: A Parent's Guide to Safe and Healthy Viewing, by Lauryn Axelrod (New Jersey: Citadel Press, 1997)

The Smart Parent's Guide to Kids' TV, by Milton Chen (San Francisco: KQED Books, 1994)

"Mommy, I'm Scared" How TV and Movies Frighten Children and What We Can Do to Protect Them, by Joanne Cantor (San Diego: Harcourt Brace, 1998)

On gender issues:

Raising Cain: Protecting the Emotional Life of Boys, by Dan Kindlon, Ph.D. and Michael Thompson, with Teresa Barker (New York: Ballantine Books, 1999)

Boys Will Be Boys, by Myriam Miedzian (New York: Doubleday, 1991)

The following books may offer more ideas:

Chalk Around the Block, by Sharon McKay and David MacLeod (Somerville House and Andrews and McMeal). Includes five chunky chalks and a holster.

Children's Games in Street and Playground, by Iona and Peter Opie (Oxford University Press)

Miss Mary Mack and Other Children's Street Rhymes, by Joanna Cole, Stephanie Calmenson and Alan Tiegreen (New York: Morrow Junior Books, 1990)

Anna Banana: 101 Jump-Rope Rhymes, by Joanna Cole (Beach Tree Books)

Red Rover, by Edith Fowke (Doubleday Canada Ltd.)

The Cooperative Sports and Games Book: Challenge Without Competition, by Terry Orlick (New York: Pantheon Books, 1978)

Bibliography

Craig, Wendy M., and Debra J. Pepler. *Contextual Factors in Bullying and Victimization*. Toronto: York University, 1992.

Craig, Wendy M., Debra J. Pepler and Jennifer Connolly. "A Cumulative Risk Model of Victimization: Educational, Physical and Psychological Health Risk Following the Transition to Adolescence," 1998.

Dale, Ronald R. "Mixed Versus Single-Sex Schools: The Social Aspect of Bullying." In *Bullying: A Practical Guide to Coping for Schools*. Ed. Michele Elliott. Harlow: Longman, 1991.

Elliott, Michele, ed. *Bullying: A Practical Guide to Coping for Schools*. Harlow: Longman, 1991.

Farrington, David P. "Understanding and Preventing

Bullying." In *Crime and Justice*, Volume 17. Ed. M. Tonry. Chicago: University of Chicago Press, 1993.

Feltham, R.F., A.B. Doyle, A.E. Schwartzman, L.A. Serbin, and J.E. Ledingham. "Friendship in Normal and Socially Deviant Children." *Journal of Early Adolescence* 5, 3 (1985): 371-382.

Hart, Craig, ed. *Children on Playgrounds*. Albany, NY: State University of New York Press, 1993.

Huesmann, L.R., L.D. Eron, M.M. Lefkowitz, and L.O. Walder. "Stability of Aggression over Time and Generations." *Developmental Psychology* 20 (1984): 1120-1134.

King, Alan J.C., and M.J. Peart. *Teachers in Canada: Their Work and Quality of Life*. Kingston: Queen's University, 1992.

King, Alan J.C., and Beverly Coles. *The Health of Canada's Youth, Views and Behaviours of 11-, 13- and 15-year-olds from 11 Different Countries*. Ottawa: Minister of National Health and Welfare, 1992.

Lyons, Judith, Lisa A. Serbin, and Keith Marchessault. "The Social Behavior of Peer-Identified Aggressive, Withdrawn, and Aggressive/Withdrawn Children." *Journal of Abnormal Child Psychology* 16, 5 (1988): 539-552.

Mathews, F. *Reframing Gang Violence*. Toronto: Central Toronto Youth Services, 1993.

————. *What's So Funny About the Abuse of Boys and Young Men?* Toronto: Central Toronto Youth Services, 1993.

————. *Youth Gangs on Youth Gangs.* Ottawa: Department of Supply and Services, 1993.

————. *Youth Gangs/Groups in Metropolitan Toronto: An Exploratory Typology.* Toronto: Central Toronto Youth Services, 1990.

Mathews, F., J. Banner, and C. Ryan. *Youth Violence and Dealing With Violence In the Schools.* Toronto: Queen's Printer, 1992.

Mellor, Andrew. *Bullying in Scottish Secondary Schools.* Edinburgh: Scottish Council for Research in Education, 1990.

Nowicki Jr., Stephen, and Marshall P. Duke. *Helping the Child Who Doesn't Fit In.* Atlanta, GA: Peachtree Publishers Ltd., 1992.

Olweus, Dan. *Aggression in the Schools: Bullies and Whipping Boys.* Washington D.C.: Hemisphere Publishing Corp., 1978.

Pal, Anita, and David M. Day. *Bullying at School: A Survey of Two Inner City Schools from the Metropolitan Toronto Separate School Board.* Toronto: Earlscourt Child and Family Centre, 1991.

Pepler, Debra, and Wendy Craig. *About Bullying—Handouts 1 and 2*. Toronto: York University.

Pepler, Debra, Wendy Craig, and W.R. Roberts. "Aggression in the Peer Group: Assessing the Negative Socialization Process." In *Coercion and Punishment in Long-Term Perspectives*. Ed. J. McCord. New York: Cambridge University Press, 1993.

Pepler, Debra J., and K.H. Rubin, eds. *The Development and Treatment of Childhood Aggression*. Hillsdale, NJ: Erlbaum, 1991.

Pepler, Debra, Wendy Craig, Suzanne Ziegler, and Alice Charach. "A School-Based Antibullying Intervention: Preliminary Evaluation." In *Understanding and Managing Bullying*. Ed. D. Tattum. Heinemann Books.

Ryan, C., F. Mathews, and J. Banner. *Student Perceptions of Violence*. Toronto: Central Toronto Youth Services, 1993.

———. *A Role for Police in the Anti-Violence Community School*. Toronto: Central Toronto Youth Services, 1993.

Schwartzman, Alex E., Jane E. Ledingham, and Lisa A. Serbin. "Identification of Children at Risk for Adult Schizophrenia: A Longitudinal Study." *International Review of Applied Psychology* 34 (1985): 363-380.

Schwartzman, Alex E., Pierrette Verlaan, Patricia L. Peters, and Lisa A. Serbin. "Sex Roles as Coercion." In

Coercion and Punishment in Long-Term Perspectives. Ed. J. McCord. New York: Cambridge University Press, 1993.

Serbin, Lisa A., Patricia L. Peters, Valerie J. McAffer, and Alex E. Schwartzman. "Childhood Aggression and Withdrawal as Predictors of Adolescent Pregnancy, Early Parenthood, and Environmental Risk for the Next Generation." *Canadian Journal of Behavioural Science* 23, 3 (1991): 318-331.

Serbin, Lisa A., Judith A. Lyons, Keith Marchessault, Alex E. Schwartzman, and Jane E. Ledingham. "Observational Validation of a Peer Nomination Technique for Identifying Aggressive, Withdrawn, and Aggressive/ Withdrawn Children." *Journal of Consulting and Clinical Psychology* 55, 1 (1987): 109-110.

Serbin, Lisa A., Keith Marchessault, Valerie McAffer, Patricia Peters, and Alex E. Schwartzman. "Patterns of Social Behavior on the Playground in 9-11-year-old Girls and Boys: Relation to Teacher Perceptions and to Peer Ratings of Aggression, Withdrawal, and Likeability." *Research Bulletin* (Concordia University, Centre for Research in Human Development) 9, 4 (1990–91).

Smith, Peter K., and David Thompson, eds. *Practical Approaches to Bullying.* London: David Fulton, 1991.

Tattum, Delwyn P. and David A. Lane, eds. *Bullying in Schools.* Stoke-on-Trent: Trentham, 1989.

Tremblay, R.E., R.M. Zhou, C. Gagnon, F. Vitaro, and H.

Boileau. "Violent Boys: Development and Prevention." *Forum on Corrections Research*, Volume E, 3 (1991), pp. 29-35.

Ziegler, Suzanne, and Merle Rosenstein-Manner. *Bullying at School: Toronto in an International Context*. Toronto: Toronto Board of Education, 1991.

Ziegler, Suzanne, Alice Charach, and Debra J. Pepler. *Bullying at School*. Unpublished manuscript, 1993.